Picture Perfect Knits

PICTURE PERFECT KNITS

Step-by-Step Intarsia with More than 75 Inspiring Patterns

By **Laura Birek**

Photographs by **Sheri Giblin**

Illustrations by **Randy Stratton**

CHRONICLE BOOKS

SAN FRANCISCO

I owe sincerest thanks to my editor, Jodi Warshaw,
for all her guidance and help in the process of writing
this book. I am also endlessly grateful to Cat Head,
Madelyn Cain, my brother and parents, and all my
friends who supported me in my knitting and writing.

Text copyright © 2008 by **Laura Birek**.
Photographs copyright © 2008 by **Sheri Giblin**.
Illustrations copyright © 2008 by **Randy Stratton**.

Manufactured in China

Designed by **Catherine Head**

10 9 8 7 6 5 4 3 2 1

Chronicle Books LLC
680 Second Street
San Francisco, California 94107
www.chroniclebooks.com

Library of Congress Cataloging-in-Publication Data:

Birek, Laura.
Picture perfect knits / by Laura Birek ;
photographs by Sheri Giblin ;
illustrations by Randy Stratton.
p. cm.
Includes index.
ISBN 978-0-8118-6068-0
1. Knitting. 2. Knitting—Patterns. I. Title.
TT820.B64165 2008
745.594'1—dc22
2007039829

CONTENTS

1

INTRODUCTION TO INTARSIA

INTRODUCTION

Just what the heck is intarsia?

Just what the heck is intarsia? In a nutshell, intarsia is a style of knitting in which you work different colored shapes or designs into a knitted piece. It's easy. It looks cool. It's totally worth your while. Best of all, you can incorporate intarsia into almost any knitting pattern.

If you're a little dubious, I don't blame you. Few knitting techniques are as universally shrouded in darkness as intarsia is. Some knitting how-to books give the technique short shrift and many pattern books ignore intarsia completely.

There are many knitters who, though they enjoy intarsia, can't find a good pattern to save their lives. I'll admit it here and now: Many intarsia patterns are kitschy and dated, and they can't even be worn for ironic value. But it need not be so! You can just as easily knit a skull and crossbones with intarsia as you can a prancing reindeer. It's just a matter of finding (or creating) pretty and cool patterns—exactly what I aim to provide for you right here in this book.

Picture Perfect Knits will show you that intarsia can be easy and beautiful. All it takes are a few simple skills, a bit of creativity, and a willingness to throw your preconceived notions out the window.

In the first section of the book I explain the basics of the technique and show you how to navigate intarsia charts and create your own patterns. Next, you'll find 10 step-by-step patterns—from an adorable dog sweater to a statement-making Che Guevara pillow. Included at back are over 50 intarsia design charts that you can use for a wide range of projects.

A brief history of intarsia

Before prancing reindeer and snowmen gave intarsia a bad name, argyle was the reigning king of the technique—the noble grandfather of all intarsia work, if you will. It showed up on the scene in the 1500s, when members of the Campbell clan of Argyll, Scotland, rocked the motif on kilts and, later, footwear. The author Sir Walter Scott had a tendency to name-drop the Argyle boys in his novels, and soon the distinctive diamond pattern became known as "argyle plaid."

In the 1940s, American women knit argyle socks en masse to send to their boys fighting overseas. Even after the GIs returned from duty, the style remained popular. And no design defined the preppy 1950s like a smart argyle vest.

Exactly when knitters took the leap from snappy argyle to what we now consider intarsia is unclear. Looking through old knitting books and magazines, you'll find a variety of intarsia styles—plaids and geometrics as well as representational motifs from the 1960s and 1970s. The 1980s was a pretty popular decade for intarsia—lots of animal, floral, and allover abstract patterns, usually in bold colors. More recently, consider the work of Kaffe Fassett, one of the best-known knit designers. His designs feature rich colors and geometric and floral motifs—a very contemporary use of intarsia.

Isn't it more trouble than it's worth?

For some reason, intarsia strikes fear into the heart of even the most seasoned knitter. The main worry is how to deal with those separate strands of yarn dangling behind your piece. I grant that the wrong side of an intarsia swatch can look a little intimidating. But you will be fine as long as you stick with the techniques described in this book. Also, because you drop the old strand when you come to a color change, you only hold one color at a time, so there's no tricky double stranding, as in Fair Isle.

Fair isle or intarsia?
What's the difference?

Both Fair Isle and intarsia are color-knitting techniques. With Fair Isle you carry your different strands of yarn behind the work, creating what we call "yarn floats." In intarsia, each separate block of color is worked with a different strand of yarn, and no strand is carried more than a few stitches.

If you compare the wrong side of a Fair Isle swatch to that of an intarsia swatch, you'll see the difference immediately. All the yarn floats in Fair Isle create a fabric that's doubly thick. Because you don't carry yarn with intarsia, the fabric is of a single thickness.

Both techniques have their place in knitting, and knowing when to use them can make or break a finished garment. Fair Isle is the best technique for small, repeating patterns with only a few stitches per color.

Traditionally, Fair Isle only uses two colors per row, while intarsia can feature as many as needed. When a chart features a large block of a second (or third, or fourth) color, it's time to use intarsia. Here's a general rule of thumb to remember: If a pattern calls for more than four stitches in a separate color, you should use intarsia.

Okay, i'm convinced. What now?

As with most things, practice makes perfect. Intarsia is no exception. It helps to knit a few swatches before jumping into a full-fledged intarsia pattern. In the following section, "Intarsia Techniques," I provide a few examples to help you get started. Next, I discuss yarn options and how to choose the right colors and textures. Once you've mastered the basic techniques, you'll be ready to dive into the full patterns or even create your own intarsia charts!

INTARSIA TECHNIQUES

Have no fear, fellow yarn junkies. You'll need to learn only a few easy techniques to master this thing we call intarsia.

THE BASICS

Before we get into the nitty-gritty, it's essential that you understand the maxim of intarsia: Avoid yarn floats at all costs. How do you spot a yarn float? It's time for show and tell.

Take your favorite Fair Isle sweater and turn it inside out. See that mess of yarn strung across the back of the colorwork? Those are yarn floats. They're finger-snagging, garment-bulking beasts, and the beauty of intarsia is that you can easily avoid these troubles.

It's really quite easy. You'll simply use a separate piece of yarn whenever you change colors. But first, you'll need to know how to navigate an intarsia chart.

HOW TO READ AN INTARSIA CHART

Before you skip to the patterns and other good stuff, try your hand at reading the test swatch to the right. In this example, gray indicates right-side rows; white, wrong-side rows. In standard intarsia charts, right and wrong side are not indicated—but here we've indicated right and wrong sides for educational purposes. The black box represents the second color of yarn you'll add using the intarsia technique. Because most intarsia is worked in stockinette stitch, you'll knit right-side rows and purl wrong-side rows.

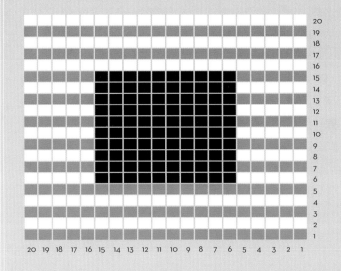

Because intarsia is worked back and forth, you must read the chart in alternating directions. Right-side rows are read from right to left. Wrong-side rows are read left to right. Each box on the grid represents one stitch. This chart shows a ten-stitch-by-ten-row intarsia rectangle motif surrounded by five stitches of the background color on each side. Reading from the bottom up, you see the second color gets added on the sixth row (a wrong-side row). The chart tells you to work the intarsia pattern for ten rows the same way: five stitches in color A, ten stitches in color B, five stitches in color A. On row sixteen the pattern ends, and you continue across in the original color for four more rows.

For some more practice, consider a slightly more complicated pattern. (This intarsia motif is also worked over twenty stitches, so you can continue on with the same swatch if you like.)

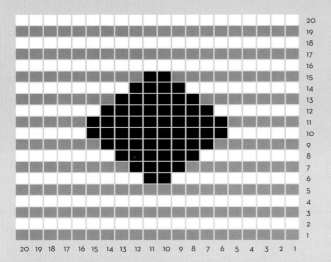

Here, the intarsia pattern also starts at row six, but this time you must work nine stitches in color A, two stitches in color B, and nine stitches in color A. For row seven, you work eight stitches in color A, four stitches in color B, and eight stitches in color A, and so on.

The final task is to determine where to add in new lengths of yarn. The rule of thumb with intarsia is that you add a new length of yarn every time you change colors in a row. Consider the first chart we looked at.

Though there are only two colors worked in this design, you will need three different strands of yarn per row to work it. On the sixth row, where you begin the intarsia pattern, you'll add a second strand in color B to begin the contrasting block on the sixth stitch. Then, to change back to the original color on stitch sixteen of the row, you must add a third strand of yarn.

On the chart, stars indicate where you add a new strand of yarn.

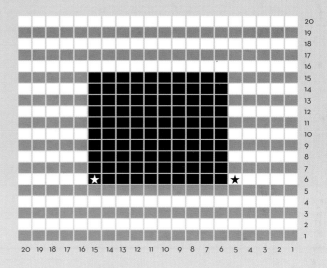

More complex designs require more strands:

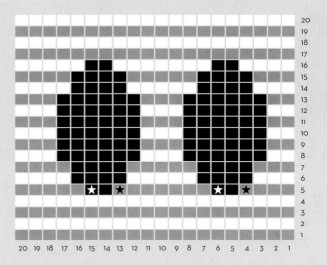

In the example above, you need five separate strands of yarn, including the orginal strand of color A. See the next page for more information on how to attach your yarn.

WORKING WITH DIFFERENT STRANDS

Attaching a new strand

So, now that you know where to add new yarn, how exactly do you do it? Unlike adding new yarn at the end of the row, you can't just start knitting with the new strand, because it will leave an unsightly gap between your stitches. Instead, you must secure the new strand of yarn to your knit fabric before starting. Some people prefer to add the new yarn by tying a knot around the old yarn one stitch before they start working the new color.

In my opinion, the best way to attach new yarn is to twist it together with the old. Knotting creates unattractive and uncomfortable lumps in your finished garment. Twisting keeps the fabric smooth and consistent. To do this, knit one stitch with the new color, and then just bring the old yarn over your working yarn and keep knitting. You'll see that this secures the new strand to the fabric just as well as tying a knot does.

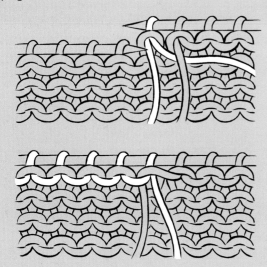

Be sure to leave at least 5 inches of tail so you can easily weave in the ends later on.

Changing colors midrow

Once you have secured the yarn by twisting, you can start working the intarsia pattern. When it comes time to change colors midrow, remember these two important steps: *twist* and *tug*.

Every time you change strands of yarn, you must *twist* them together to prevent a hole from forming between your stitches. Without the twists, you'd be knitting two separate pieces side by side. As outlined above, when you attach a new strand, knit one stitch with the new color; then lay the old strand over your working yarn and continue knitting. When you change colors midrow, you twist *before* beginning knitting with the new color. It's only necessary to twist the strands once to secure the yarn. As you knit a few more rows, you will begin to see the twisted stitches on the wrong side.

Almost as important as twisting is gently *tugging* on your yarn every time you change colors. After you knit your first stitch in the new color, gently pull on the last two stitches one at a time. This ensures that the stitches stay snug and don't balloon out or get misshapen. As you progress in your knitting, you may notice a stitch loosening or a gap forming. A gentle tug on the dangling ends should fix this problem. If the gap persists, don't worry; you can fix it during the finishing process described on page 16.

Carrying yarns

When a color in your intarsia chart jumps more than four stitches, you usually have to attach a new strand. On occasion, however, you can carry the yarn behind your work and continue knitting. The way to do this is to wrap the carried yarn around your working yarn every other stitch. For example, if you need to jump five stitches, knit one in color A, twist color B behind the working yarn, knit two more stitches, twist again, and knit two more stitches. Now you're ready to begin knitting with color B and you don't have to add a new strand!

Twisting

Some knitters get confused by the term "twisting." One way to think of the twist is that you're always laying the old yarn over the new yarn, locking them together. As you knit more rows, the yarns naturally alternate being on top, and thus they become twisted or woven together on the wrong side.

Step-by-step quick reference for adding a new strand of yarn

1. Knit final stitch in color A.
2. Knit new stitch in color B.
3. Bring color A strand over color B.
4. Knit next stitch in color B.
5. Gently tug on both strands.

Wait! I lost my place on the chart!

Inevitably, at some point all intarsia knitters suddenly find themselves with a horrible sinking feeling. They've lost their place on the chart. Is this a disaster? Is it necessary to rip out your work and start again? Nope. A chart is an exact representation of what you're knitting. This means you can both read from the chart to find out what to do next and read from your knitting to find out what you've just done.

If you've lost your place, check out your knitting on the right side. Look for a distinctive spot in the pattern—for instance, where the contrasting color has increased or decreased—and count the number of rows you've knit since that point, including the stitches on your needle. Then count up from the same point on the chart; that will be the row you just knit. Easy as pie.

To avoid this whole mess in the first place, mark the row you're working on. One way to mark your row is to use sticky notes. Once you've finished a row, just restick the note on the chart and carry on. Another option is to make a photocopy of the pattern and, with a pen or highlighter, mark off the rows as you knit them.

EXCEPTIONS TO THE RULE

As we've learned, the whole point of intarsia is to avoid yarn floats, but what happens when you have to make one stitch here or there in a contrasting color? Rather than adding a new strand of yarn just for one or two stitches, you can fib your way through the chart.

The most-used technique is the duplicate, or cover, stitch. This stitch intends to simply cover or duplicate other stitches after the fact. To work a duplicate stitch, cut a manageable length of yarn and thread it through a tapestry needle. Starting at the base of the first stitch you want to cover, thread the needle through the exact same gaps that the knitting follows (see figures on the next page). Duplicate stitch is most notably used to create those diagonal lines you see in classic argyle patterns.

If you're working an intarsia pattern and there's just one stitch of the contrasting color in a row, consider using this little cheat: If you need the same color as is used in the row below, you can slip the stitch and carry on knitting the rest of the piece. This will carry the color up from the row below, and, though it's still technically one stitch, it'll appear to span two rows in the final knit project. Just don't slip stitches too often or it may create unsightly puckers in your knit fabric.

Step 1

Step 3

Step 5

Step 2

Step 4

Step 6

Yarn, bobbins, butterflies, and loose ends

Now that you've mastered adding new strands and twisting, you'll need a way to keep all your strands in order.

Yarn
Here's a simple trick to help you estimate how much yarn you'll need for an intarsia motif. If you're working with a small intarsia chart, count the number of stitches used for the color you're concerned about. Then take the yarn and wrap it ten times loosely around your knitting needle. This is approximately the length you'll need for ten stitches. Multiply this length by as many tens of stitches as you have in your motif (overestimating is always best), and then add ten inches for weaving in the ends. If you're working with a larger chart, you can either estimate how many stitches you'll use, or just use shorter strands and add in new ones as needed.

Bobbins
When working with intarsia, you can quickly become tangled in what seems like hundreds of dangling strands of yarn. To avoid a migraine, you'll need to find a way to manage all your yarn strands.

Traditionally, knitters have used yarn bobbins to manage multiple strands. To use a bobbin, simply wind your yarn around and dangle it behind your knitting. As you need more yarn, you can pull it out of the bobbin's slotted end. You can find bobbins in almost any craft or yarn store.

Alternatively, you can make your own bobbins from clothespins (see figure on next page) or even from scrap cardboard. To create a cardboard bobbin, cut a rectangle with a wide notch on one side and a notched opening on the other. For sport- and worsted-weight yarns, a good size for a homemade bobbin is approximately 3 inches by

1 inch. Of course, bulky yarns require larger bobbins, while lace-weight yarns call for smaller ones.

Though bobbins keep yarn strands neat and tidy, they have a few drawbacks. The other yarns can snag on the bobbin, which can be horribly frustrating when you are trying to navigate a complicated intarsia chart. Bobbins may also slow you down because you have to unwind more yarn almost every row.

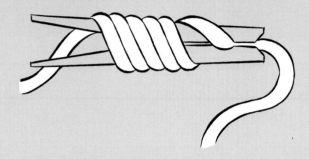

Butterflies

Butterflies are perfect for the minimalists out there. The beauty of butterflies is that they require no additional hardware while still keeping your strands orderly. To make a butterfly, spread your index and middle fingers and wrap the length of yarn around them. When you have about 8 inches left, create a loop (as you would for a slip knot) and wrap it around the yarn. Carefully slip your fingers out of the yarn and pull on the end to secure. When you need more yarn from the butterfly, simply open the loop, pull out more yarn, and resecure the butterfly.

Though butterflies are less susceptible to snagging than bobbins, the yarn can still become tangled and slow you down.

Loose ends: Let 'em hang

This is a technique that is gaining favor among knitting bloggers and professional designers alike. Neatly avoiding bobbins and butterflies, this freewheeling method involves using shorter lengths of yarn (no longer than 60 inches) and letting them hang loose behind the knitting. As you switch colors, you simply grab the yarn you need from the bunch of loose yarns and keep knitting. When you run out of a certain color, just cut another manageable length and add it in. If the ends begin to tangle, you'll likely be able to simply comb out the snarls with your fingers.

The downside to letting your strands hang loose is that you end up with extra yarn ends to weave in at the end because you are knitting with shorter lengths. However, if weaving in ends doesn't bother you, then this might be the method for you. I prefer to use a combination of butterflies and loose yarn ends. I butterfly the larger sections and use hanging short lengths for the smaller motifs.

Why can't I just use whole balls of yarn?

Good question. It seems like the logical thing to do, right? But this idea quickly loses its charm when you actually try to knit intarsia using full balls of yarn. Because the balls of yarn are so large, they quickly become twisted and tangled. Unlike bobbins, butterflies, or even loose shorter strands of yarn, full skeins are not easily untangled. If that doesn't convince you, consider this: If you use whole balls, you'll have to buy tons more yarn!

FINISHING

Weaving in ends

So, you've finished working your intarsia chart and the right side looks gorgeous. But what to do about the mess on the wrong side? Even the simplest intarsia motifs leave you with dangling yarn ends to weave in. Unfortunately, there's no way to get around this task, but at least you can make quick work of it. The main thing to remember is this: Weave in both directions. This means that if you begin weaving the ends in to the right, finish by weaving back to the left. This will keep the ends from unraveling and making you cry.

You can use either a tapestry needle or a crochet hook to weave in hanging ends. The crochet hook works best if your ends are shorter, while the tapestry needle will give you more control over where your yarn goes. It is also important to try to weave ends into knitting of the same color. It's not always possible, but if you keep colors together you won't mar your beautiful intarsia work with peekaboo strands.

While weaving in ends from the intarsia work, you may notice some small gaps between your stitches. You can kill two birds with one stone by fixing these while weaving in ends. Simply wrap the strand you're weaving in around the gap and pull it snug. Continue weaving in the end as normal and the hole will disappear.

Blocking

After weaving in your ends, cover stitching as needed, and closing any gaps in the fabric, you must block your knitting. I know, I know: Blocking is boring, you say. It gets my yarn all wet and then it takes forever to dry, you cry. I have nowhere to do it, you complain. What's the point anyway?

Here's the raw deal: Blocking takes a misshapen fabric and turns it into a perfectly formed, finished object. It smoothes out all the uneven stitches that are often a nasty side effect of intarsia work. It also can help mold your knitting to the right size and shape, even if that doesn't seem possible. The best blocking tutorial I've found was written by Eunny Jang on her blog, See Eunny Knit. You can find the link to this tutorial in the "Resources" section (page 128).

Here is the boiled-down version of wet blocking:

1. Wash your knits according to the yarn labels' care instructions.
2. Extract as much water from the knits as possible without wringing the fabric. Then lift the fabric from the water, supporting the weight of the item from underneath.
3. Lay your knits out on a towel on a flat, scratch-proof surface.
4. Using rustproof pins, pin all sides of the fabric to your desired dimensions. Let dry.

When you're finished with this process, you'll find the fabric transformed.

See? Intarsia isn't such a scary monster after all. Once you know how to read a chart, twist and tug, and keep your yarn in check, intarsia will seem as easy as Sunday morning.

CHOOSING YARN

Picking out the right yarn may be the most important step in intarsia. However, with so many colors, fibers, textures, and gauges available, choosing a yarn can sometimes be overwhelming. Where to start? Read on.

Color

First, you'll want to decide which colors to use. Most fiber companies offer color charts for each yarn they produce, which can be a huge help in narrowing down a yarn choice, especially if you'll be knitting with more than two or three colors.

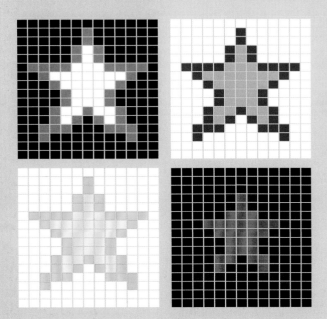

When picking a color combination, think about whether you want the intarsia pattern to be prominent or subtle. Choosing yarns close in hue, tone, or value can create a subtle pattern, while contrasting, highly saturated colors can make a pattern really pop. You can make the same chart look completely different just by knitting with different colors.

When buying yarn, it's always important to check the dye lot on the label. This number indicates skeins that were dyed together and thus have the exact same color. Yarns with different dye lots can look similar in the store but horrifyingly different once you get them home. Unless you're aiming for a two-toned piece, stick with yarn from the same dye lot.

Fiber and texture

Another factor to consider when planning an intarsia project is the fiber and texture of the yarn. Animal fibers, whether 100 percent or blended with a synthetic, tend to be the most forgiving. Because the wrong side of the intarsia work has many ends woven in, using a yarn with a little spring and give can make it much easier to hide mistakes. Plant fibers, such as cotton or bamboo, have less elasticity and can be a bit more finicky. I recommend knitting with a slightly smaller needle than suggested if you're using plant fibers. This will give your fabric a bit more coverage and help prevent yarn ends from peeking through.

If you're working an intricate pattern, you should use smooth yarn. Smooth yarns will enhance each stitch and display your intarsia work in detail. On the other end of the spectrum are fuzzy novelty yarns. These yarns will hide your individual stitches and create a texture that's almost like faux fur. If you're aiming to make a plush object with large, undetailed motifs, a novelty yarn will work really well. Mohair and other brushed yarns fall in between the smooth and novelty categories; they create a knit fabric with some stitch definition and a bit of a foggy haze.

If you're feeling adventurous, why not try mixing textures? You might knit the main part of a piece with smooth yarn but make an intarsia motif (perhaps a large heart) in fuzzy novelty yarn. The resulting fabric will have a charming three-dimensional quality.

Gauge and density

Gauge is an essential element of a knitting pattern. The label on a skein will tell you the predicted gauge of a given yarn when knit with a specific needle size. These are just guidelines, however, and you can manipulate the look and feel of your finished object by changing the needle size or using more than one strand of yarn at a time.

To create a lacier fabric, just increase the needle size until you get the desired effect. Similarly, if you want to tighten up the fabric, try smaller needles. You can also create a bulkier fabric by knitting with two strands of yarn at the same time. Just double the millimeter size of the needles called for on the yarn label and you'll be knitting twice as fast! This method is best used on patterns you've designed yourself, since doubling the yarn essentially doubles the gauge and makes the finished object twice as big!

For intarsia, a slightly tighter gauge is usually preferable. This helps ensure that contrasting color yarn doesn't show through on the right side. You can, however, experiment with gauge to create a unique piece. If you knit the majority of a piece in bulky-weight yarn, and then knit the intarsia chart in sport-weight yarn, you will create a lacy, semi-see-through area. The downside of knitting lacy intarsia is that there's nowhere for your yarn ends to hide. If you try this method, make sure to sew the ends into the tighter-gauge fabric.

However you decide to play with gauge and texture, be sure to make a swatch before you start your project. This will eliminate any nasty surprises and ensure that the finished piece will fit properly.

CREATING PATTERNS

Now that you've got this intarsia thing all sewn up, are you looking for a new challenge? How about creating your own intarsia charts? You can convert almost any image to a knitting chart, but you'll need to learn some special tricks before pulling out your knitting needles.

CREATING AN INTARSIA CHART

Yarn aspect ratios

When it comes time to chart out a pattern, most knitters immediately pull out a quad-ruled notebook. Though these notebooks were trusty biology-lab companions in school, normal graph paper is actually not the best choice for creating knitting charts. This is because knitted stitches are generally wider than they are tall. This means a knit pattern charted on conventional graph paper will knit up looking compressed, sort of like what you see in a fun-house mirror.

Here's a simple solution: Use knitter's graph paper. I've included a general-use chart at the end of this book that you can photocopy and use for your designs. You'll also find many resources online that will make customized graph paper depending on your yarn's gauge. I've listed a few of these links in the "Resources" section (page 128), but a Web search for "knitter's graph paper" will also do the trick.

Gauge, chart size, and image complexity

The next thing to decide is how large you want your motif to be. The main limiting factor for chart size is your knitting gauge and the item you want to knit. For example, if you want to make a scarf in bulky wool, you'll generally cast on no more than 20 stitches, so your intarsia chart will need to be 20 stitches or fewer in width. In contrast, a sweater knit in sock-weight yarn can accommodate charts of 100 or more stitches.

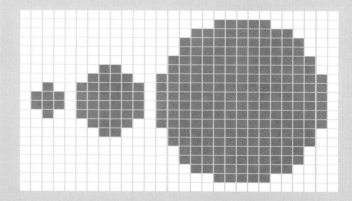

The more stitches you have available, the more complex the intarsia pattern can be. And fewer stitches in a chart require a simpler design. It's similar to the concept of resolution quality in digital images: More megapixels allow you to see more detail.

Types of images

When picking images for intarsia charts, you might find that it helps to think of them in terms of pixels. In everyday life, we're used to seeing objects and pictures with smooth edges. But with intarsia, every image has to fit into a grid, or get "pixelated."

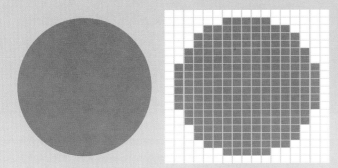

The simpler the image, the easier it is to adapt it to a knitting chart. Also, it's helpful to choose images that have clear edges and strong lines.

Don't forget to consider color when you're charting out an image. How many colors do you want to use in your knitting? Using more than three colors at a time can make knitting difficult and expensive. Before adding several colors to your piece, consider the following:

1. For every new color, you'll need to buy a separate ball of yarn.
2. For every color change, you'll have to knit with a separate piece of yarn.
3. Your chosen yarn must come in all the colors you choose. Check the manufacturer's color charts before you become wedded to a certain color arrangement.

Hand-drawing charts

The most egalitarian way to create intarsia charts is simply to print out the knitter's graph paper or photocopy the blank grid on page 119 and start drawing. You can draw basic shapes and then fill in the squares along the edges of your illustration.

Another option is to print the graph paper onto transparency sheets. Then you can lay the graph over any image you want to convert to an intarsia chart. The downside of working with paper is that, once you've made a mistake, it's difficult to erase. Also, it can be less precise than working with a computer program.

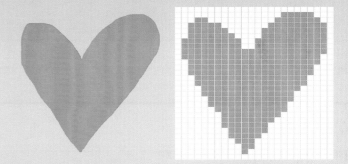

Computer programs

Several Mac and PC computer programs are available for creating knitting charts. I use Cochenille's Stitch Painter. Using this software, you can copy and paste images into the charts as well as draw freehand. Many software companies offer free trials to help you decide whether a program is right for you. I've listed links to popular knitting programs in the "Resources" section (page 128).

CHOOSING A PROJECT

Though intarsia can be added to almost any knitting pattern, not all knitting projects are suited for intarsia work. There are a few guidelines to keep in mind when creating your own knitting patterns with intarsia.

The first consideration is whether the piece will have a visible wrong side. Because intarsia work usually leaves you with a lot of yarn ends to weave in, the wrong side of intarsia charts often looks a little messy. Knitting patterns that keep their wrong sides private are best suited for intarsia work.

Scarves are the most commonly knitted objects with a visible wrong side. In this book, I provide a pattern for a scarf with pockets that hides the wrong side of the intarsia chart. Another option for making an intarsia scarf is to make two panels and sew them together on all sides. Luckily, most knitting patterns are designed to have a hidden wrong side. Sweaters, pillows, bags, iPod cozies, and hats are all fair game for intarsia work.

Consider whether the knitting pattern is worked flat or in the round. Traditional intarsia can only be worked flat, so patterns worked in the round must be modified when you are adding an intarsia chart. Or, if the intarsia chart you'd like to add is small enough, you could work it in afterward using the duplicate or cover stitch.

Your final decision will be where to place the intarsia design on your knitting. A central location is a good choice for a chart that fills most of the knit fabric, or if you want the design to be the main focus of the piece. However, offset designs can be very dramatic. Consider placing a repeating motif around the hem, neckline, or sleeves. Just try to avoid placing an important design too close to the seam where it won't be seen. Similarly, try to avoid underestimating the length of a piece and then being unable to finish the chart. If you take the time to know your gauge and sketch (or even chart!) your pattern ahead of time, these heartbreaks can be prevented.

INTARSIA IN THE ROUND

As mentioned previously, intarsia patterns are traditionally knit flat, alternating knit and purl rows and turning at the end of every row.

Strictly speaking, there's no way to do *true* intarsia in the round. To mimic the look of intarsia in the round, you have to either fake the intarsia or fake knitting in the round—you can't do both simultaneously. If you're working in the round, you have to either carry the yarn behind the colorwork or attach a new strand for each row. If you're working intarsia, you have to turn your work every row and join the rows to make the piece look like it was knitted in the round. Both ways are, in my opinion, more trouble than they're worth. With good seaming, a flat-knit piece can look just as good (or better), and it saves you the grief of figuring out a new technique while you're already learning intarsia. If you absolutely, positively want to use intarsia when knitting in the round, an Internet search will produce instructions for various techniques.

2

FULL PROJECT PATTERNS

JOLLY ROGER

Skull-and-Crossbones Pocket Scarf

Looking for a project to get you started? This scarf is perfect for intarsia beginners. Graphic pockets at each end enhance a simple garter-stitch scarf. Putting the intarsia on the pockets hides the wrong sides. As an added bonus, the scarf won't have any yarn loops to snag fingers on. You'll knit the pockets and scarf separately and then sew them together. I've used a skull-and-crossbones motif for this pattern, but you can use any intarsia chart smaller than 30 stitches wide and 48 stitches tall.

Finished measurements

- Length: 66 inches
- Width: 6.5 inches

Materials

- Lion Brand Wool-Ease Worsted Weight (80% acrylic / 20% wool; 85g = 197 yds)
- Main Color (MC): black, 2 skeins
- Contrasting Color (CC): fisherman, 1 skein
- Size 8 (5mm) needles (or size needed to match gauge)
- Tapestry needle
- Straight pins

PATTERN

Scarf:

- With MC, CO 30 sts.
- Knit all rows (garter stitch) until scarf measures 66 inches.
- BO all sts.

Pockets (make 2):

- CO 30 sts with MC.
- Purl 1 row.
- Begin working intarsia chart in stockinette stitch.
- Work to end of chart: 48 rows.
- BO all sts.

GAUGE

- 18 sts and 24 rows per 4 inches

FINISHING

Using tapestry needle, sew in all ends on pocket panels and scarf. Place one pocket at one end of the scarf, making sure that the crossbones are at the bottom edge of the scarf. Temporarily secure pocket in place at all four corners using pins, clips, or scrap yarn. Using a length of MC yarn and top-stitching along the edge, sew the two sides and the bottom of the pocket to the scarf. Sew in ends. Repeat with other pocket, making sure it's sewn on to the same side of the scarf as the other pocket and is oriented properly so the skulls will be right-side up when you wear the scarf.

OLD SCHOOL

FELTED ARGYLE BAG

Argyle is the quintessential and most traditional use of intarsia. This felted tote has a vintage flair not only in its argyle motif but also in its funky combination of 1960s-worthy colors. You'll knit this bag double-stranded on large needles, making it a quick and easy project. The felting process creates a dense and sturdy fabric, which, when combined with a wide strap, makes for a durable book bag.

FINISHED MEASUREMENTS

Before felting:

- Panels: 21 inches wide by 25 inches tall
- Gusset and strap: 5 inches wide by 120 inches long

After felting:

- Panels: 16 inches wide by 13 inches tall
- Gusset and strap: 3 inches wide; strap will be about 38 inches long

MATERIALS

- Lion Brand Lion Wool (100% wool; 85g = 158 yds)
- Main Color (MC): lemongrass, 6 skeins

PATTERN

PANEL 1 (BACK):

- With 2 strands of MC held together, CO 63 sts.
- Work in stockinette stitch, starting with a purl row, until panel measures 25 inches from cast-on edge.
- BO all sts.

PANEL 2 (FRONT):

- With 2 strands of MC held together, CO 63 sts.
- Begin working intarsia chart in stockinette stitch.
- *Note: the stripes can be added by duplicate stitch after completing the pattern.*
- When panel measures 25 inches from CO edge, BO all sts.

GUSSET AND STRAP:

- *Note: The right side of the gusset is the side where the color change is not "smooth" but staggered.*

- Contrasting Color 1 (CC1): pumpkin, 4 skeins
- Contrasting Color 2 (CC2): goldenrod, 4 skeins
- Size 11 (8mm) needles (or size needed to match gauge)
- Tapestry needle
- Safety pins or extra yarn scraps
- Washing machine, pillowcase, and rubber band
- Shoebox and rags (optional)

Gauge

12 sts and 14 rows per 4 inches in stockinette stitch before felting (with 2 strands held together)

- With 2 strands of CC1 held together, CO 15 sts.
- * Knit 6 rows (garter stitch) with CC1. Switch to CC2 and knit 6 rows.
- Switch to CC1. Repeat from * until gusset measures 120 inches from CO edge.
- BO all sts.

FINISHING

Connect Ends of Gusset:

- With a tapestry needle, sew the ends of the gusset together, forming a loop, making sure not to twist the strap.

Secure Panels for Seaming:

- With the right sides facing out, carefully safety pin or tie panels to the gusset securing each corner, making sure to match the front and back panels to the same rows of the gusset. Place the seam of the gusset at the center bottom of the panels. Secure the panels as needed to ensure easy seaming.

Sew Seams:

- With a single strand of MC, sew the front panel to the gusset along three sides, removing pins or ties as you progress. Repeat with the back panel.

Sew in Ends:

- Securely sew in ends, including those from seaming and the intarsia work.

Felting Instructions:

- Follow the manufacturer's felting instructions, or felt according to the directions below.

- Place the bag inside a pillowcase secured with a rubber band, or a zippered lingerie bag, to prevent damage to your washing machine. Set the machine for a small load and a hot wash, and add the bag and a small amount of soap. When done, check the piece for size. You may need to run the wash cycle several times before the bag reaches the desired size. Make sure to check the strap for length—it may require extra felting. To felt strap separately, fill a sink with hot, soapy water and agitate strap by hand until it is felted to the right length.

After felting, remove excess water by pressing bag between two towels. Optionally, mold to shape by placing a shoebox in the bottom of the bag and padding with extra rags or dishtowels. Remove shoebox once fabric is dry.

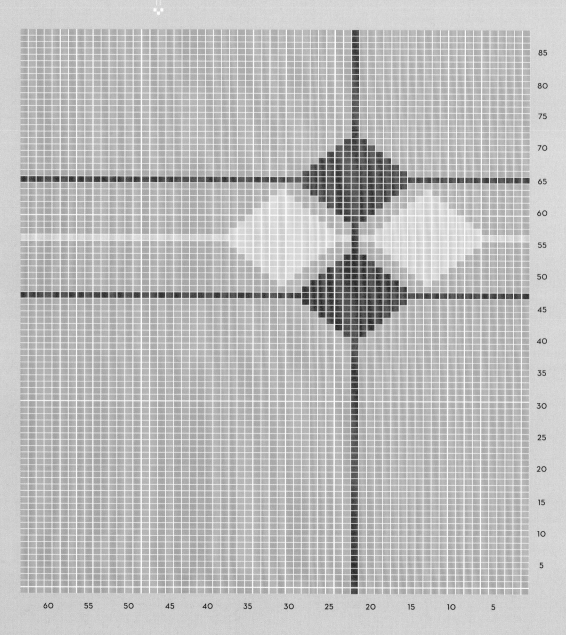

HEARTS AND BONES

Dog Sweater
BY CATHERINE HEAD

As if your canine buddy isn't cute enough already, here comes the ultimate in swoon-inducing dog sweaters. With a ribbed turtleneck, intarsia hearts-and-bones repeating motif, and front-leg sleeves, this sweater will turn your best friend into the best-dressed pup at the park.

Size

One size; fits medium-sized dogs

Finished measurements

22.5 inches long; 22-inch circumference

Materials

Brown Sheep Lamb's Pride Superwash Worsted (100% washable wool; 100g = 200 yds)

Main Color (MC): cactus, 2 skeins

Contrasting Color 1 (CC1): alabaster, 1 skein

Contrasting Color 2 (CC2): rose quartz, 1 skein

Size 8 (5mm) 24-inch circular needles (or size needed to match gauge)

Pattern

Collar:

The collar is worked in 2x2 ribbing, increasing 1 on each side every fourth row as follows:

With MC, CO 64 sts. Do not join. The sweater is worked flat and then seamed up the belly.

Row 1: (K2, P2) to end.

Rows 2–3: Repeat row 1.

Row 4: K1, m1, K1, (P2, K2) to last 2 sts, P1, m1, P1.

Row 5: P1, (K2, P2) to last st, K1.

Rows 6–7: Repeat row 5.

Row 8: P1, m1 (K2, P2) to last st, m1, K1.

Rows 9–11: (P2, K2) across.

Row 12: P1, m1, P1, (K2, P2) to last 2 sts, K1, m1, K1.

Rows 13–15: K1 (P2, K2) to last st, P1.

Row 16: K1, m1 (P2, K2) to last st, m1, P1.

Rows 17–24: Repeat rows 1–8. (76 sts on needle)

The body is worked in stockinette stitch.

- Size 8 (5mm) double-pointed needles (for sleeves)
- Tapestry needle
- 2 stitch markers

GAUGE

- 18 sts and 20 rows per 4 inches in stockinette stitch

BODY:

- **Row 25 (WS):** Purl, increasing 1 stitch at center of row. (77 sts)

Begin shaping the body:

- **Row 26 (RS):** K1, m1, K to last 2 sts, m1, K1. (79 sts)

- **Row 27:** P7, place marker, P to last 7 sts, place marker, P to end. There are 65 sts between markers.

- **Row 28:** K1, m1, K to marker, work intarsia pattern between markers, K to last st, m1, K1. (81 sts)

- **Row 29:** P across.

- **Rows 30–33:** Repeat rows 28–29 twice. (85 sts)

- **Row 34:** Repeat row 28. (87 sts)

- **Row 35–36:** Repeat rows 25–26. (89 sts)

Make the armholes as follows:

- **Row 37:** P12, join new yarn, BO 3 sts, P59, join new yarn, BO 3 sts, P12. You will work each of the three sections separately for 12 rows. (83 sts)

- **Row 38:** K1, m1, K to end of section, (13 sts); K59; K to last st, m1, k1. (13 sts)

- **Row 39:** P across.

- **Rows 40–49:** Repeat Rows 38–39 5 more times. (18 sts on each side and 59 sts in center section)

Finish armholes and rejoin sections into a single piece, continuing with one strand of yarn only.

- **Row 50:** K18, CO 3 sts, K59, CO 3 sts, K18. (101 sts)

- **Rows 51–63:** Work even in stockinette stitch.

Shape lower back:

- **Rows 64–65:** BO 6 sts, work to end of row. (89 sts)

- **Rows 66–67:** BO 4 sts, work to end of row. (81 sts)

- **Row 68–69:** BO 3 sts, work to end of row. (75 sts)

- **Row 70:** K1, k2tog, K to last 3 sts, k2tog, K1. (73 sts)

- **Row 71:** P1, p2tog, P to last 3 sts, p2tog, P1. (71 sts)

- **Rows 72–73:** Repeat rows 70–71. (67 sts)

- **Row 74:** Repeat row 70. (65 sts)

- **Rows 75-80:** Begin working intarsia chart while repeating rows 72-73 three times. (53 sts)
- **Rows 81-83:** Work even in stockinette stitch and finish intarsia chart.
- **Row 84:** Repeat row 70. (51 sts)
- **Rows 85-92:** *Work 3 rows even, then repeat Row 70, repeat from * twice more. (45 sts)
- **Rows 93-110:** Work even in stockinette stitch.
- BO all sts.

STRAPS (MAKE 2):

- Pick up 4 stitches on right rear edge of sweater body.
- K 40 rows (garter stitch).
- BO all sts.
- Sew loose end to the right side where the body decreases began.
- Repeat to make a second strap and sew onto left side.

SLEEVES (MAKE 2):

- With DPNs, pick up 32 sts around right armhole.
- Work in K2, P2 ribbing for 11 rounds. BO loosely.
- Repeat for left sleeve.

FINISHING

- Sew in all loose ends.
- Sew body together from the CO edge to where the body decreases began.

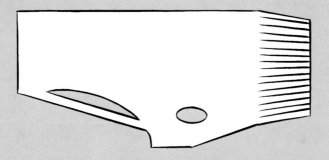

Sweater Shape

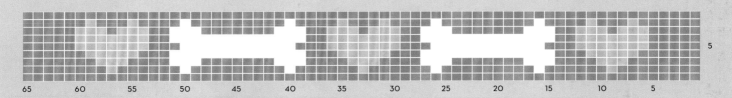

Collar-end intarsia chart

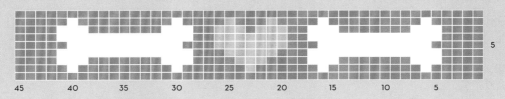

Hind-end intarsia chart

ARMCHAIR REVOLUTIONARY

THROW PILLOW

★

Ever wonder what it would be like to have Che Guevara in your living room? With this 14-inch pillow, you can always have him on hand. The pattern comes with options for either a fabric or a knitted back, and, because the wrong side is hidden inside the pillow, the intarsia motif requires little finishing. Remember that you can use duplicate stitch rather than intarsia to add in small details, if you prefer.

FINISHED MEASUREMENTS

14 by 14 inches

MATERIALS

- Koigu Premium Merino Solids (100% merino wool; 50g = 175 yds)
- Main Color (MC): true red, 1 skein
- Contrasting Color 1 (CC1): deep brown, 1 skein
- Contrasting Color 2 (CC2): white, 1 skein
- Size 3 (3.25mm) knitting needles (or size needed to match gauge)
- 2 stitch markers
- Tapestry needle
- Straight pins

PATTERN

FRONT:

- With MC, CO 100 sts.
- Work 8 rows in stockinette stitch (starting with a knit row).
- Begin working the intarsia pattern. K10 sts, place marker, work row 1 of the intarsia chart over the next 80 sts, place marker, K to end of row. From now on, work the intarsia chart between the stitch markers.
- Work the remaining 109 rows of the intarsia chart in stockinette stitch.
- After finishing the chart, work 8 additional rows in stockinette stitch with MC.
- BO loosely.

BACK (KNIT OPTION):

- With color of your choosing CO 100 sts.
- Work even in stockinette stitch for 124 rows, or until piece measures 14 inches.
- BO loosely.

For knit-back option, you will need:

- 1 additional skein in desired color

For cloth-backed option, you will need:

- ½ yard fabric (45-inch width)
- Sewing machine or sewing needle and thread

Gauge

- 28 sts and 36 rows per 4 inches

Whipstitch

Also known as an overcast stitch. With wrong sides together, bring the needle and thread through both pieces of fabric from the back to the front. Move the needle 1/4" along your edge and bring the needle back through both pieces from the back to the front again. Continue in this manner until your seam is complete.

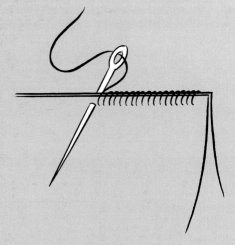

Back (Fabric Option):

- Cut fabric into 2 square panels measuring 15 by 15 inches.
- With right sides together, sew around edges with a ½-inch seam, leaving a 2-inch opening. Turn panels right sides out and topstitch along opening.

FINISHING

- Use duplicate stitch to cover any color work missed while knitting the intarsia.
- Weave in ends. It isn't critical to sew in every end, because they will be hidden inside the pillow, but make sure you close any gaps and sew in any ends that might come loose.
- Block your knit pieces so they measure 14 by 14 inches. Once dry, pin front and back pieces around the pillow form with right sides out. With CC2 (or the color of your choice), whipstitch securely around all 4 sides of the pillow. Sew in ends.

I ♥ MOM

Baby Sweater

Ever wonder what to make for the vegan, environmentalist baby in your life? This sweater, made from 100 percent bamboo yarn, is the perfect gift. The bamboo yarn has a great drape, and you'll impress all your friends with how you've turned panda food into fashion.

Size

- 6–12 months (1–2, 2–3 years)

Finished measurements

- 20 (24, 26) inch chest circumference

Materials

- Rowan Classic Yarns Bamboo Soft (100% bamboo; 50g = 112 yds)
- Main Color (MC): cambria, 4 (5, 5) skeins
- Contrasting Color 1 (CC1): turberose, 1 skein
- Contrasting Color 2 (CC2): cream, 1 skein
- Contrasting Color 3 (CC3): gypsum, 1 skein
- Size 5 (3.75mm) and size 3 (3.25mm) needles (or size needed to match gauge)

Pattern

Back:

- With MC and smaller needles, CO 62 (74, 82) sts.
- Work in 1x1 rib for 1 inch.
- Change to larger needles and work even in stockinette stitch until piece measures 10 (12, 13) inches from CO edge.
- BO all sts.

Front:

- With MC and smaller needles, CO 62 (74, 82) sts.
- Work in 1x1 rib for 1 inch.
- Change to larger needles and work even in stockinette stitch until piece measures 4.5 (6.5, 7.5) inches, ending with a WS row.
- Begin working intarsia chart:
- K 12 (18, 22) sts, place marker, work row 1 of intarsia chart, place marker, K 11 (17, 21) sts.
- Continue working intarsia chart between markers.

- Tapestry needle
- 2 stitch markers

Gauge

- 25 sts and 30 rows per 4 inches in stockinette stitch with larger needle

When piece measures 7.5 (9.5, 10.5) inches from CO edge, begin shaping neckline:

K 25 (31, 35) sts, attach second ball of yarn, BO center 12 sts, K 25 (31, 35) sts.

Work both sides of neckline at the same time.

* P across.

K to last 3 sts before neckline, k2tog, k1. Change yarns. K1, skp, k across.

Repeat from * 9 more times. 40 (52, 60) sts.

Work even until piece measures 10 (12, 13) inches from CO edge.

BO all sts.

Sleeves (make 2):

With MC and smaller needles, CO 42 (48, 52) sts.

Work in 1x1 ribbing for 1 inch.

Change to larger needles and begin working in stockinette stitch.

* K1, m1, K to last st, m1, K1.

P across.

K across.

P across.

Repeat from * 9 (12, 15) times. 62 (74, 82) sts.

Work even in stockinette stitch until sleeve measures 6.5 (7.5, 8.5) inches from CO edge.

BO all sts.

FINISHING

Sew shoulder seams.

With MC and smaller needles, pick up 74 (80, 86) sts evenly along neckline.

Work in 1x1 rib for 1 inch. BO loosely.

Sew sleeves to body. Sew side seams and under sleeves.

Weave in all ends.

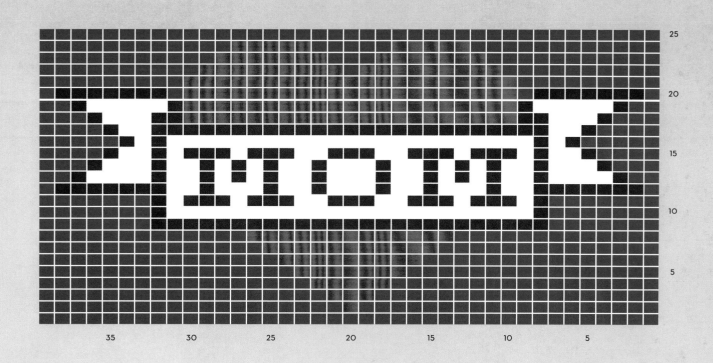

KITTEN MITTENS

Knit flat with bulky yarn and then seamed, these mittens are a quick and easy project. The intarsia pattern is small and simple, making this a perfect project for the intarsia novice. And these mittens are machine-washable, so the little wild animal in your life can get messy without ruining her paws!

SIZE

- Child's size M (L, XL)

FINISHED MEASUREMENTS

- Palm circumference of 5.5 (6, 6.5) inches to fit ages 3–4 (4–5, 5–6)

MATERIALS

- Lion Brand Jiffy (100% acrylic; 85g = 135 yds)
- Main Color (MC): white, 1 skein
- Contrasting Color (CC): dusty pink, 1 skein
- Size 7 (4.5mm) and size 8 (5mm) straight needles (or size needed to match gauge)
- Stitch holder
- Tapestry needle

PATTERN

(Make 2, following right mitten chart for the first and left mitten chart for the second.)

- With MC and smaller needles, CO 22 (24, 26) sts.
- Work K1, P1 ribbing for 6 (6, 8) rows.
- Change to larger needles and begin working in stockinette stitch.
- K6 (7, 8), kfb, K8, kfb, K6 (7, 8). 24 (26, 28) sts.
- P across.
- K11 (12, 13), kfb, kfb, K11 (12, 13). 26 (28, 30) sts.
- P across.
- K11 (12, 13), kfb, K2, kfb, K11 (12, 13). 28 (30, 32) sts.
- P across.
- K11 (12, 13), kfb, K4, kfb, K11 (12, 13). 30 (32, 34) sts.
- P across.
- K11 (12, 13), kfb, K6, kfb, K11 (12, 13). 32 (34, 36) sts.
- P12 (13, 14), place next 8 sts on holder, with same strand of yarn pulled taut, P12 (13, 14). 24 (26, 28) sts.
- K0 (1, 2), work row 1 of intarsia chart, K0 (1, 2).

Gauge

16 sts and 22 rows per 4 inches with larger needles in stockinette stitch

Continue working intarsia chart in stockinette stitch.

On final row of chart, begin fingertip shaping: K1, skp, K7 (8, 9), k2tog, skp, K7 (8, 9), k2tog, K1. 20 (22, 24) sts.

P across.

K1, skp, K5 (6, 7), k2tog, skp, K5 (6, 7), k2tog, K1. 16 (18, 20) sts.

P across.

K1, skp, K3 (4, 5), k2tog, skp, K3 (4, 5), k2tog, K1. 12 (14, 16) sts.

P across.

BO all sts, leaving a long tail of yarn.

Thumb:

With right side facing, pick up 1 (1, 2) sts on right edge of thumb hole, K8 sts from holder onto larger needles, and pick up 1 (1, 2) st on other edge of hole. 10 (10, 12) sts.

Work thumb even in stockinette stitch for 2.5 (3, 3) inches, ending with a WS row.

K2tog 5 (5, 6) times.

Cut yarn, leaving a long tail, and, with a tapestry needle, thread end of yarn through stitches. Drop stitches off needle and pull taut.

FINISHING

With long tail from BO, sew sides of mitten together using mattress stitch. Use the same method to seam down the center of the thumb, making sure to close any gap formed at the base of the thumb. Weave in all ends.

Right Mitten

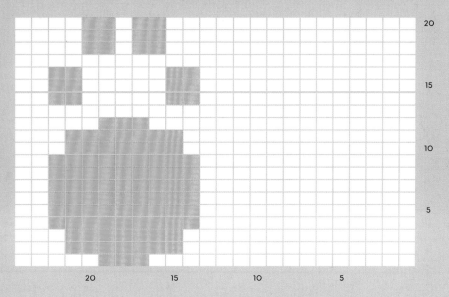

Left Mitten

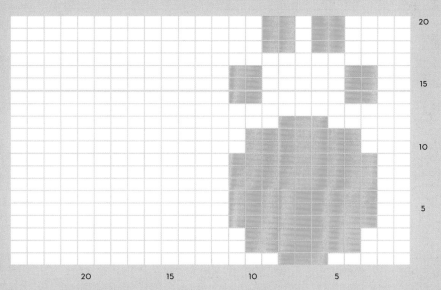

KITTY HAT

This *chapeau* is for those who want the full transformation to feline-hood. And because it uses the same yarn, this is the purrfect companion to the Kitten Mitten pattern (page 46).

SIZE

- Toddler (Child, Woman, Man)

FINISHED MEASUREMENTS

- 16 (18, 20, 22) inch head circumference

MATERIALS

- Lion Brand Jiffy (100% acrylic; 85g = 135 yds)
- Main Color (MC): white, 1 skein
- Contrasting Color (CC): dusty pink, 1 skein
- Size 7 (4.5mm) and size 8 (5mm) straight needles (or size needed to match gauge)
- Tapestry needle

GAUGE

- 16 sts and 22 rows per 4 inches with larger needles in stockinette stitch

PATTERN

HAT:

- With MC and smaller needles, CO 64 (72, 80, 88) sts.
- Work K1, P1 ribbing for 1 inch.
- Switch to larger needles, K1, m1, K to last 2 sts, m1, K1. 66 (74, 82, 90) sts.
- Work even in stockinette stitch until piece measures 5 (5.5, 6, 6.5) inches.
- Shape crown:
- K1, (K6 (7, 8, 9), k2tog) 8 times, K1. 58 (66, 74, 82) sts.
- P 1 row.
- K1, (K5 (6 7, 8), k2tog) 8 times, K1. 50 (58, 66, 74) sts.
- P 1 row.
- K1, (K4 (5, 6, 7), k2tog) 8 times, K1. 42 (50, 58, 66) sts.
- P 1 row.
- K1, (K3 (4, 5, 6), k2tog) 8 times, K1. 34 (42, 50, 58) sts.
- P 1 row.
- K1, (K2 (3, 4, 5), k2tog) 8 times, K1. 26 (34, 42, 50) sts.
- P 1 row.
- K1, (K1 (2, 3, 4), k2tog) 8 times, K1. 18 (26, 34, 42) sts.

P 1 row.

K1, (K0 (1, 2, 3), k2tog) 8 times, K1. 10 (18, 26, 34) sts.

P 1 row.

For Toddler's size, skip to end of Hat pattern and cut yarn.

K1, (K- (0, 1, 2), k2tog) 8 times, K1. - (10, 18, 26) sts.

P 1 row.

For Child's size, skip to end of Hat pattern and cut yarn.

K1, (K- (-, 0, 1), k2tog) 8 times, K1. - (-, 10, 18) sts.

P 1 row.

For Women's size, skip to end of Hat pattern and cut yarn.

K1, (K- (-, -, 0), k2tog) 8 times, K1. - (-, -, 10) sts.

P 1 row.

Cut yarn. With a tapestry needle, thread yarn through all 10 sts. Drop sts off needle and pull yarn taut.

EARS:

(Make 2, following right ear chart for the first and left ear chart for the second.)

With MC and larger needles, CO 20 sts.

P 1 row.

Begin working intarsia chart.

On row 5 of chart K1, skp, K5, k2tog, skp, K5, k2tog K1, while maintaining intarsia pattern. 16 sts.

P 1 row.

K1, skp, K3, k2tog, skp, K3, k2tog, K1. 12 sts.

P 1 row.

K1, skp, K1, k2tog, skp, K1, k2tog, k1. 8 sts.

P 1 row.

K1, sk2p, sk2p, K1. 4 sts.

Cut yarn, thread yarn through 4 remaining sts. Drop sts off needle and pull yarn taut.

FINISHING

- Sew seam of hat and seams of ears using mattress stitch. Stuff a bit of scrap yarn into the pouch created by the ear. Using a length of MC, secure ears to top of hat, making sure the ears are spaced evenly from back seam and facing to the front. Weave in all ends.

Right Ear

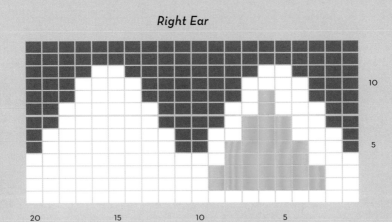

Left Ear

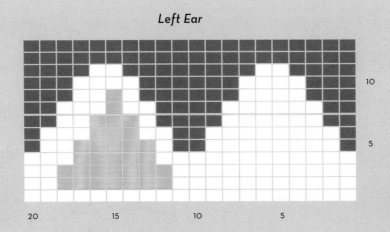

GEEK CHIC

ARGYLE VEST

Anyone with half a brain knows that nerds are cool. Show off your geek pride with this modern, sexy argyle vest. Because the argyle pattern is so easy to follow, this vest knits up quickly with little stress. And because the diagonal lines are added after knitting, you only have to worry about two colors at a time!

SIZE

- XS (S, M, L, 1X, 2X)

FINISHED MEASUREMENTS

- 28 (32, 36, 40, 44, 48) inch chest circumference

MATERIALS

- Knit Picks Telemark (100% Peruvian wool; 50g = 103 yds)
- Main Color (MC): chestnut, 5 (6, 7, 8, 9, 9) skeins
- Contrasting Color 1 (CC1): northern green, 2 (3, 3, 4, 4, 5) skeins
- Contrasting Color 2 (CC2): lichen, 2 (2, 2, 2, 3, 3) skeins
- Size 2 (2.75mm) 16- and 24-inch circular needles
- Size 4 (3.5mm) 24-inch circular needles (or size needed to match gauge)

PATTERN

BACK:

- With CC2 and smaller 24-inch circular needles, CO 76 (86, 98, 106, 118, 130) sts.
- K1 (K2, P2) to last st, P1. Repeat this step for 1 inch.
- Increase 9 (11, 11, 13, 13, 15) sts evenly across as follows: K3 (6, 9, 5, 11, 9), m1, (K8, m1) 8 (10, 10, 12, 12, 14) times, K3 (6, 9, 5, 11, 9).
- Switch to larger needles, and begin working in stockinette stitch with MC.
- Work 1 RS row.
- * Work 9 rows.

Begin waist shaping:

- The numbers apply to all sizes.
- Decrease row: K1, skp, K to last 3 sts, k2tog, K1*.
- Repeat *_* 5 more times.
- * Work 9 rows.
- K1, m1, K to last 3 sts, m1, K1. *
- Repeat *_* 5 times.

- Tapestry needle
- Straight pins

GAUGE

- 24 sts and 30 rows per 4 inches with larger needles in stockinette stitch

- Work even in stockinette stitch until piece measures 14 (14.5, 15, 15.5, 16, 16) inches from CO edge.

- BO 3 (6, 6, 9, 9, 9) sts at beginning of the next two rows.

- Work even in stockinette stitch until piece measures 23 (23.5, 24.5, 26, 27, 28) inches from CO edge.

- BO all sts.

FRONT:

- Work first 3 steps (through first series of increases) as for back.

- Switch to larger needles and begin working intarsia chart in stockinette stitch. To center argyle diamonds, begin working from stitch 15 (9, 3, 14, 8, 1) of the chart.

Begin waist shaping:

- Continue working argyle pattern from chart, and at the same time, work steps 5 to 13 (from "Work 1 RS row" through "BO 3" rows) as for back, remembering to keep chart lined up as you decrease and increase.

- When piece measures 15 (15.5, 16, 16.5, 17, 17) inches, begin neck shaping.

- K32 (38, 42, 47, 51, 55), BO 21 (21, 25, 25, 29, 35), K32 (38, 42, 47, 51, 55). Work both sides of neckline at once.

Note: Because each argyle diamond uses a different strand of yarn, there is no need to attach another ball of yarn for binding off.

- * BO 2 sts at neck edge 4 (5, 5, 6, 7, 8) times.

- Work one WS row.

- On left side of neck, K to last 3 sts before neckline, k2tog, K1, on right side of neckline K1, skp, K across. *

- Repeat *_* 11 (10, 12, 14, 16, 18) times.

- Work even until piece measures 23 (23.5, 24.5, 26, 27, 28) inches from CO edge.

- BO all sts.

FINISHING

- With CC2 and tapestry needle, cover stitch diagonal lines over argyle diamond pattern. Weave in all ends. With tapestry needle and lengths of MC, sew shoulder and side seams.

NECKLINE:

- With smaller 16-inch circular needles, pick up 200 (200, 220, 244, 268, 296) sts evenly along neckline. Work K2, P2 ribbing in the round for 1 inch. BO all sts.

ARMHOLE EDGING:

- With smaller 16-inch circular needles, pick up 112 (120, 124, 144, 148, 160) sts evenly around armhole opening. Weave in ends.

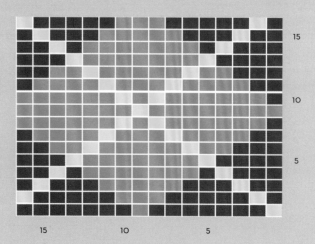

SWEET TREAT

FELTED CUPCAKE CUSHION
BY CATHERINE HEAD

Rest your head on this sweet, low-calorie treat! Knit with bulky yarn and then lightly felted, this pillow will satisfy any home decorator's sweet tooth!

FINISHED MEASUREMENTS

- 16 inches by 16 inches by 3 inches

MATERIALS

- Brown Sheep Lamb's Pride Bulky (85% wool, 15% mohair; 113g = 125 yds)
- Main Color (MC): creme, 2 skeins
- Contrasting Color 1 (CC1): Victorian pink, 1 skein
- Contrasting Color 2 (CC2): oatmeal, 20 yds
- Contrasting Color 3 (CC3): ruby red, 10 yds
- Size 11 (8mm) needles (or size needed to match gauge)
- Tapestry needle
- 1 bag polyester fiberfill
- Brown beads for sprinkles (optional)

PATTERN

BACK:

- The back panel is worked in stockinette stitch.
- With MC, CO 42 sts.
- Work 70 rows.
- BO all sts.

FRONT:

- The front panel is worked in stockinette stitch.
- With MC, CO 42 sts.
- Work 5 rows.
- Work 2 rows in CC1.
- Work 20 rows in MC.
- Begin intarsia chart. Work intarsia chart for 21 rows.
- Work 14 rows in MC.
- Work 2 rows in CC1.
- Work 5 rows in MC.
- BO all sts.

Cotton thread and sewing needle to sew sprinkles (optional)

Gauge

- 10 sts and 16 rows per 4 inches before felting

Side Panel:

- With CC2, CO 8 sts.
- Work even in stockinette stitch until piece measures 64 inches, or length needed to wrap around all 4 sides of panels.
- BO all sts.

FINISHING

- Using blanket stitch and with right-sides together, attach side panel to front and back panels. When attaching the back panel, leave a 5-inch opening on the bottom seam to allow for stuffing.
- Weave in all ends.
- Follow the manufacturer's felting instructions or see felting instructions on page 31. Wring out excess water and let bag dry completely.
- Optionally, sew sprinkles onto top of cupcake using cotton thread.
- Stuff pillow with polyester filler.
- Sew opening closed.

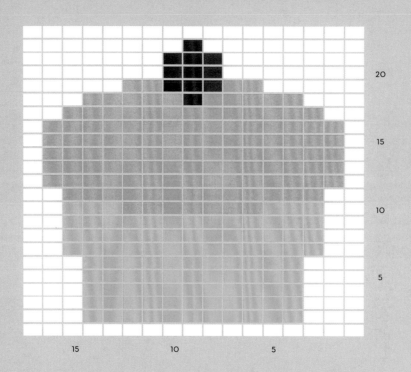

SNOWFLAKE

BY CATHERINE HEAD

Nobody will give you the cold shoulder when you're wearing this snowflake-decorated cropped cardigan. Knit with bulky wool, this shrug knits up in a jiffy—perfect for last-minute holiday gifts.

SIZE

- Girls' size 8-10 (12-14, women's small, medium, large, 1x)

FINISHED MEASUREMENTS

- 28 (32, 36, 40, 44, 48) inch chest circumference

- 14 (14.5, 14.75, 15, 15.25, 15.5) inches long

MATERIALS

- Brown Sheep Lamb's Pride Bulky (85% wool, 15% mohair; 113g = 125 yds)

- Main color (MC): charcoal heather, 4 (4, 5, 6, 7, 8) skeins

- Contrasting color (CC): white frost; 1 skein

- Size 11 (8mm) needles (or size needed to match gauge)

- Size L (8mm) crochet hook

- Tapestry needle

PATTERN

BACK:

- With MC, CO 43 (49, 55, 61, 67, 73) sts.

- K5 (8, 11, 14, 17, 20) place marker, K33, place marker, K to end of row.

- *Note: These markers will later mark the beginning and end of the intarsia chart worked on the upper back.*

- Work even in stockinette stitch until piece measures 6 (6.5, 6.25, 6, 5.75, 5) inches, ending with a WS row.

Begin armhole shaping:

- BO 2 (2, 3, 4, 5, 5) sts at beginning of next 2 rows. 39 (45, 49, 53, 57, 63) sts.

- Next row (RS): K1, skp, K to last 3 sts, k2tog, K1. 37 (43, 47, 51, 55, 61) sts.

- Next row (WS): P across.

- Repeat these 2 rows 0 (1, 2, 3, 4, 5) more times. 37 (41, 43, 45, 47, 51) sts.

- When the back measures 9 (9.5, 9.75, 10, 10.25, 10.5) inches from CO edge, begin working intarsia chart.

- Work even until piece measures 14 (14.5, 14.75, 15, 15.25, 15.5) inches from CO edge.

- BO all sts.

GAUGE

- 12 sts and 16 rows per 4 inches in stockinette stitch

RIGHT FRONT:

- CO 12 (15, 18, 21, 24, 27) sts and purl 1 row.
- Row 1 (WS): P across.
- Row 2 (RS): K1, m1, K across.
- Row 3 (WS): Purl to last st, m1, P1.
- Repeat the last 2 rows 3 more times.
- Repeat Row 2 once more. 21 (24, 27, 30, 33, 36) sts.
- Work even in stockinette stitch until piece measures 5 (5.75, 6, 6.25, 6.5) inches, ending with a RS row.

Begin armhole shaping:

- Next row (WS): BO 2 (2, 3, 4, 5, 5) sts, P to end. 19 (22, 24, 26, 28, 31) sts.
- Next row (RS): K to last 3 sts, k2tog, K1. 18 (21, 23, 25, 27, 30) sts.
- Next row (WS): P across.
- Repeat these 2 rows 0 (1, 2, 3, 4, 5) more times. 18 (20, 21, 22, 23, 25) sts.

Shape Neck:

- When piece measures 9 (9.5, 9.75, 10, 10.25, 10.5) inches from CO edge, begin shaping neckline on a RS row:
- Next row (RS): K1, skp, K across. 17 (19, 20, 21, 22, 24) sts.
- Next row (WS): P across.
- Repeat these 2 rows 8 more times. 9 (11, 12, 13, 14, 16) sts.
- Work even until piece measures 14 (14.5, 14.75, 15, 15.25, 15.5) inches from CO edge.
- BO all sts.

LEFT FRONT:

- CO 12 (15, 18, 21, 24, 27) sts and purl 1 row.
- Row 1 (WS): P across.
- Row 2 (RS): K to last st, m1, K1.

- Repeat Row 2 once more. 21 (24, 27, 30, 33, 36) sts.
- Work even in stockinette stitch until piece measures 5 (5.75, 6, 6.25, 6.5) inches, ending with a WS row.

Begin armhole shaping:

- Next row (RS): BO 2 (2, 3, 4, 5, 5) sts at beginning of next row, K to end. 19 (22, 24, 26, 28, 31) sts.
- Next row (WS): P across.
- Next row (RS): K1, skp, K to end. 18 (21, 23, 25, 27, 30) sts.
- Repeat these 2 rows 0 (1, 2, 3, 4, 5) more times. 18 (20, 21, 22, 23, 25) sts.

Shape neck:

- When piece measures 9 (9.5, 9.75, 10, 10.25, 10.5) inches from CO edge, begin shaping neckline on a RS row:
- Next row (RS): K to last 3 sts, k2tog, K1. 17 (19, 20, 21, 22, 24) sts.
- Next row (WS): P across.
- Repeat these 2 rows 8 more times. 9 (11, 12, 13, 10, 11) sts.
- Work even until piece measures 14 (14.5, 14.75, 15, 15.25, 15.5) inches from CO edge.
- BO all sts.

Sleeves (make 2):

- With MC, CO 24 (26, 28, 28, 32, 34) sts.
- Switch to CC, K across.
- Switch back to MC and begin sleeve shaping:
- Work 3 rows in stockinette stitch, beginning with a purl row.
- Next row (RS): K1, m1, K to last st, m1, K1.
- Repeat the increase row every 4th row 4 (0, 3, 5, 5, 10) more times, then every 6th row 7 (10, 8, 7, 7, 4) times. 48 (48, 52, 54, 58, 64) sts.
- Continue even until piece measures 16.5 (17, 17, 17.5, 17.5, 18) inches, ending with a RS row.

Shape sleeve cap:

- BO 2 (2, 3, 4, 5, 5) sts, at the beginning of the next 2 rows. 44 (44, 46, 46, 48, 54) sts.

- Next row (WS): P across.

- Next row (RS): K1, skp, K to last 3 sts, k2tog, K1.

- Repeat these 2 rows 0 (1, 2, 2, 3, 4) more times. 42 (40, 40, 40, 40, 44) sts.

- Next row (WS): P1, p2tog, P to last 3 sts, p2tog, P1.

- Next row (RS): K1, skp, K to last 3 sts, k2tog, K1.

- Repeat these 2 rows 5 (4, 4, 4, 4, 5) more times. 18 (20, 20, 20, 20, 20) sts.

- BO 2 sts at the beginning of the next 2 (4, 4, 4, 4, 4) rows. 14 (12, 12, 12, 12, 12) sts.

- Next row: P across.

- BO all sts.

FINISHING

- Weave in ends. With MC and tapestry needle, sew shoulder seams. Sew sleeves to body, then sew side and sleeve seams.

- With CC and size L hook, single-crochet around entire edge of body.

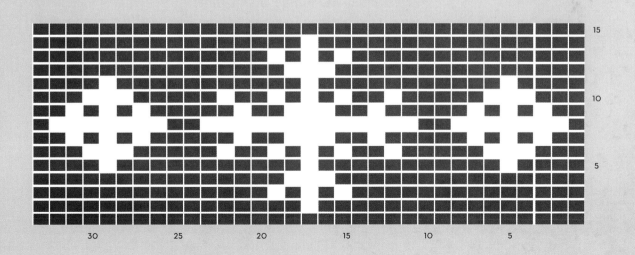

2

STAND-ALONE INTARSIA CHARTS

ABCDEFGHIJ
KLMNOPQRS
TUVWXYZ

abcdefg
hijklmno
pqrstuv
wxyz

90
85
80
75
70
65
60
55
50
45
40
35
30
25
20
15
10
5

70   65   60   55   50   45   40   35   30   25   15

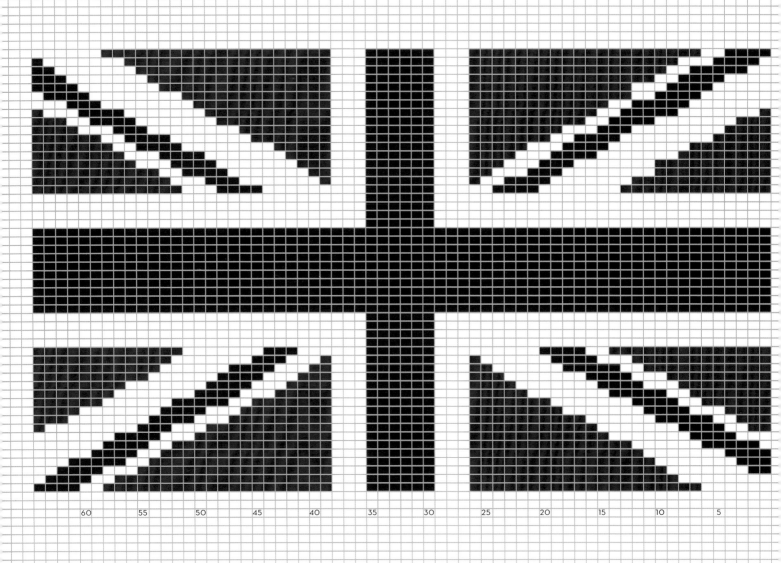

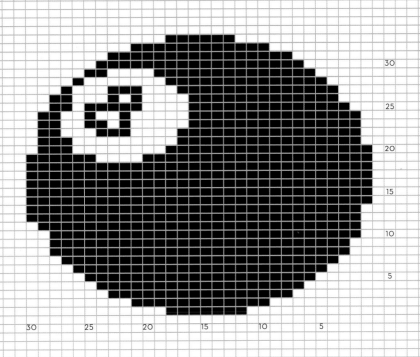

30

25

20

15

10

5

30   25   20   15   10   5

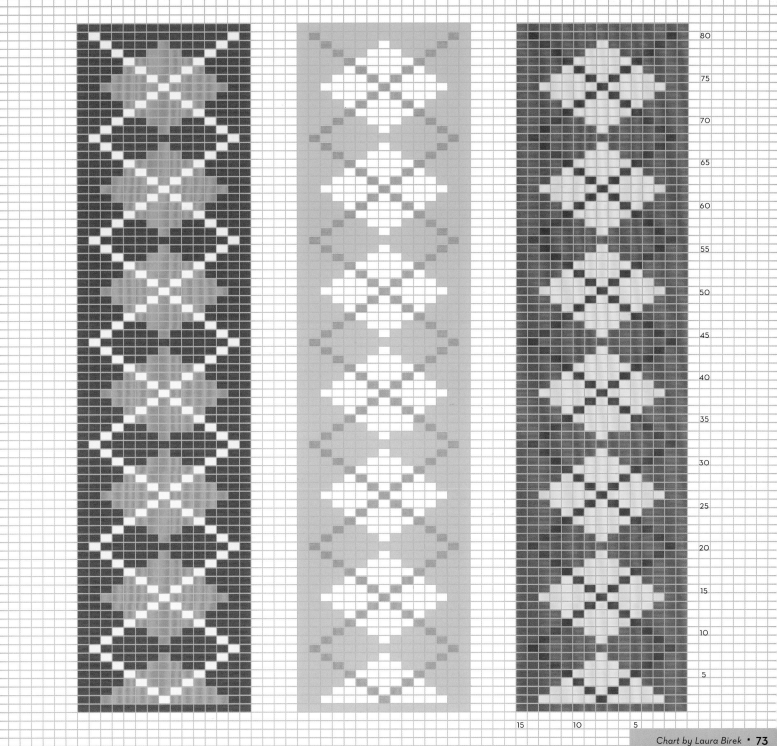

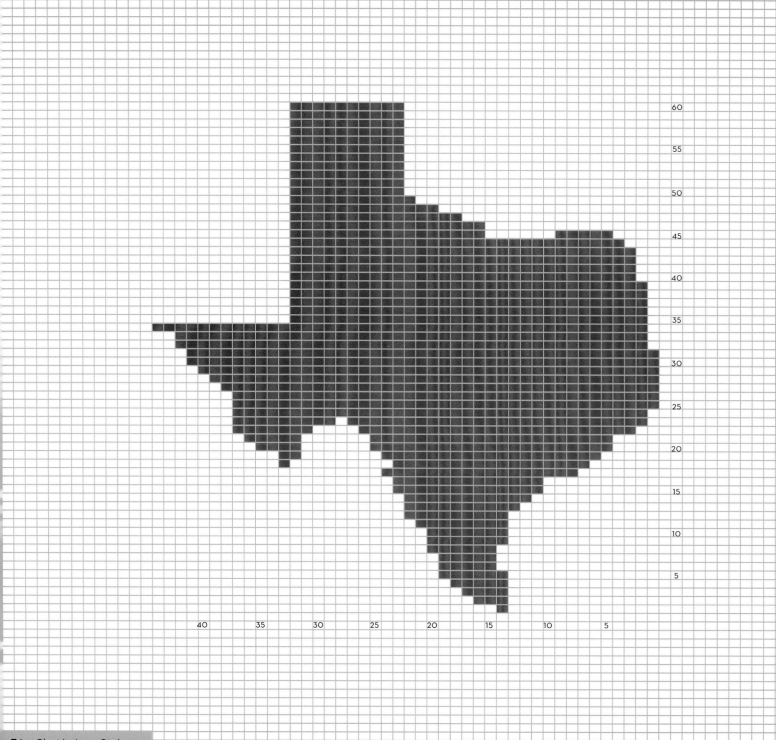

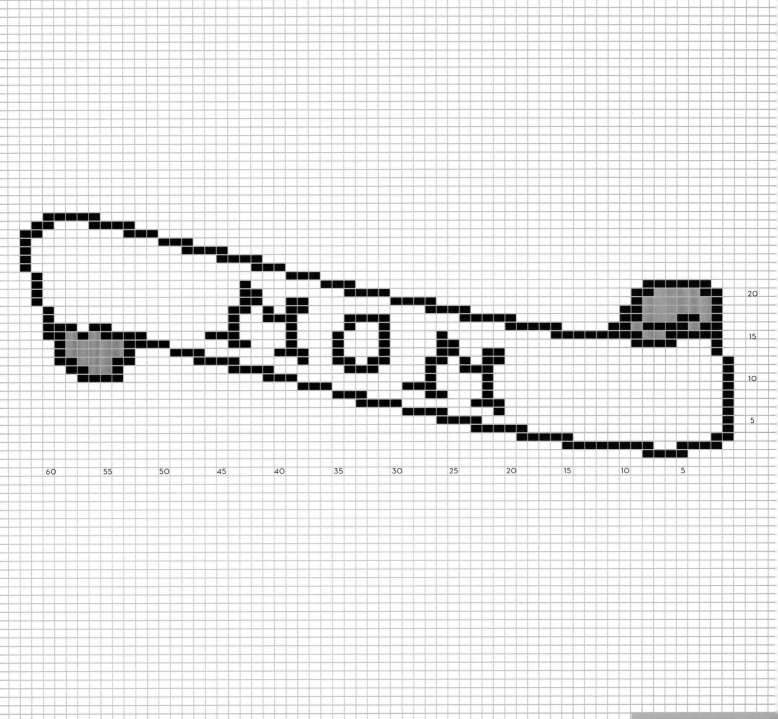

20

15

10

5

60   55   50   45   40   35   30   25   20   15   10   5

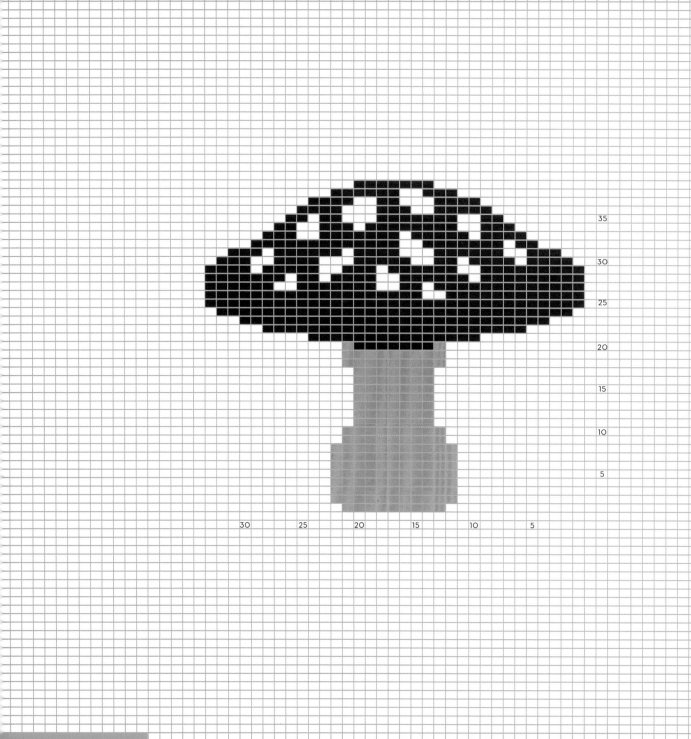

35

30

25

20

15

10

5

30   25   20   15   10   5

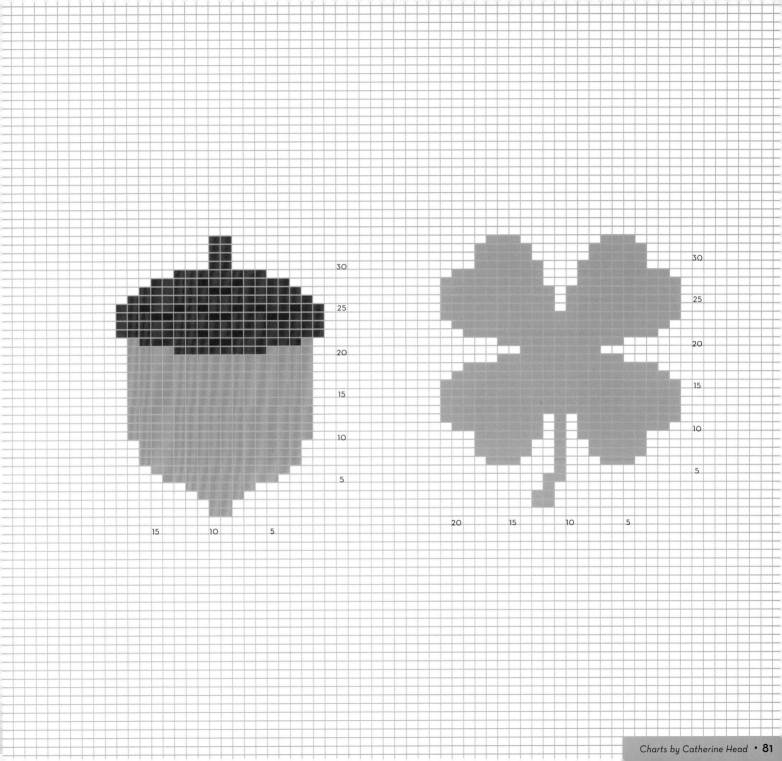

30

25

20

15

10

5

15   10   5

30

25

20

15

10

5

20   15   10   5

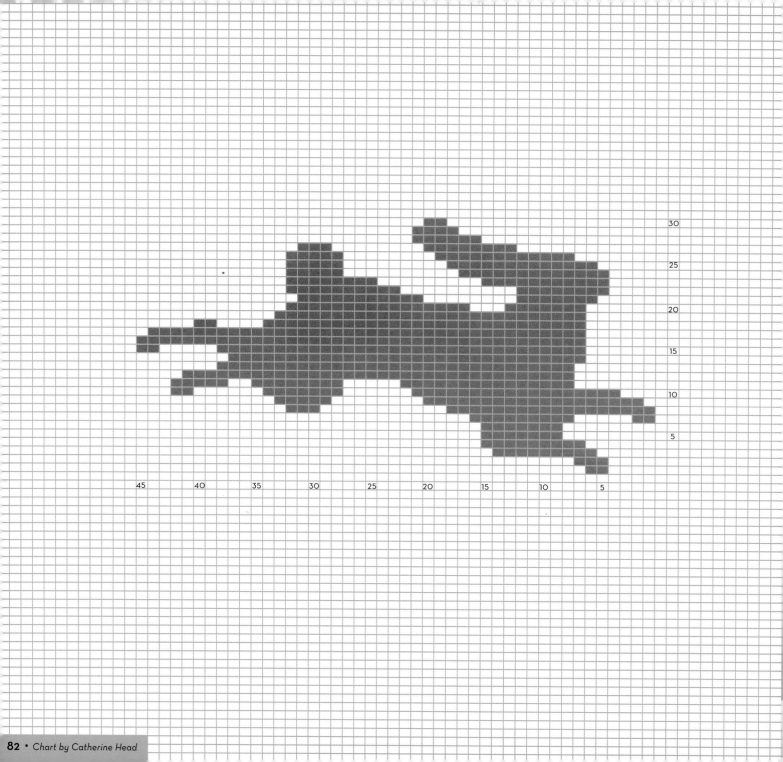

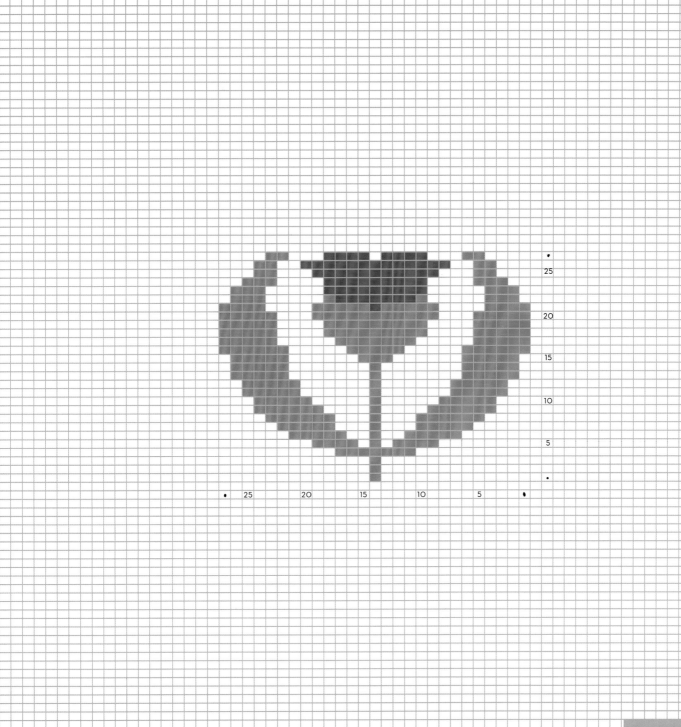

25

20

15

10

5

25 20 15 10 5

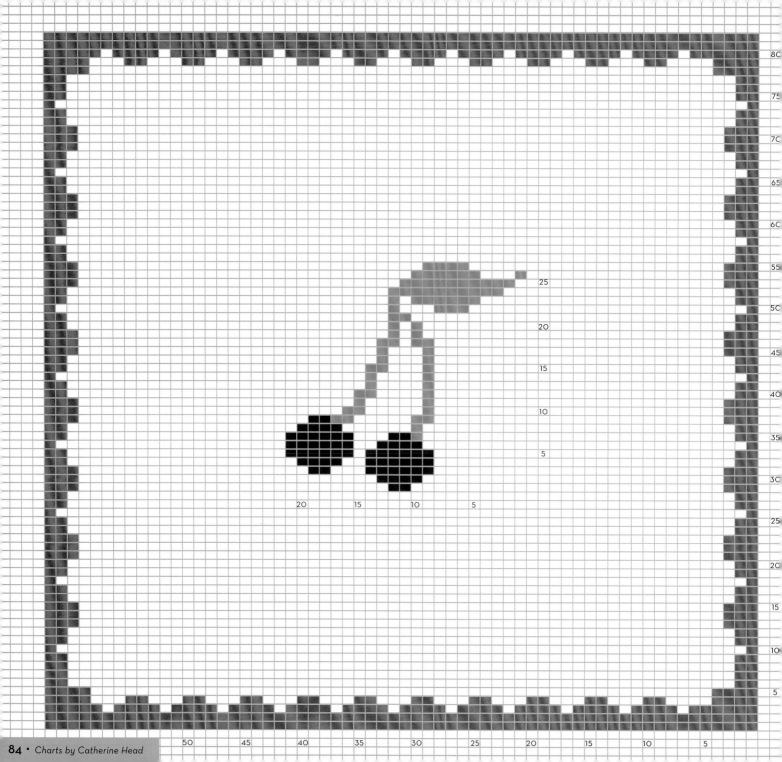

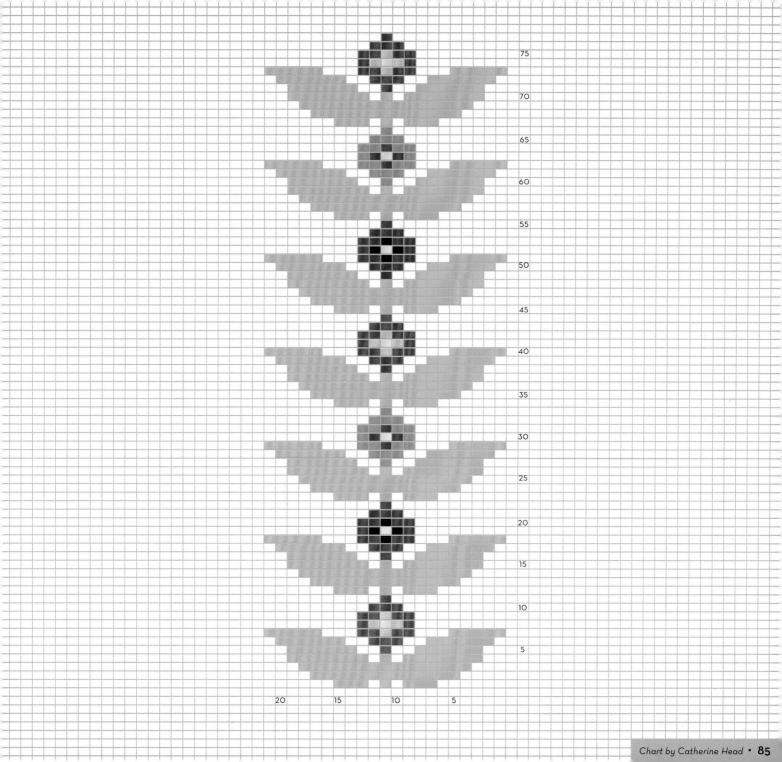

75

70

65

60

55

50

45

40

35

30

25

20

15

10

5

20   15   10   5

35

30

25

20

15

10

5

50   45   40   35   30   25   20   15   10   5

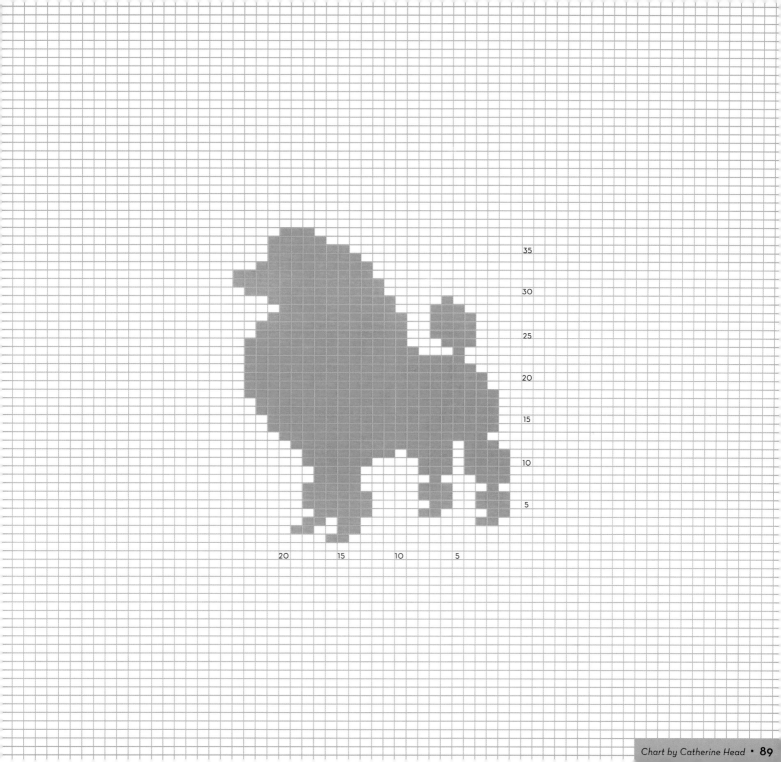

35

30

25

20

15

10

5

20   15   10   5

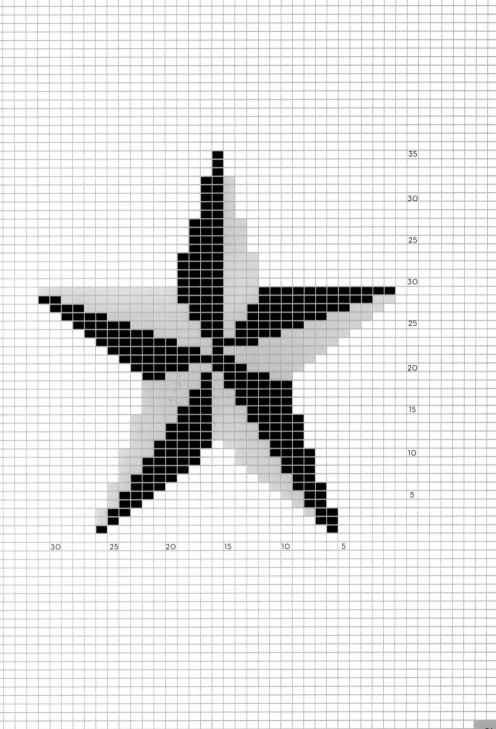

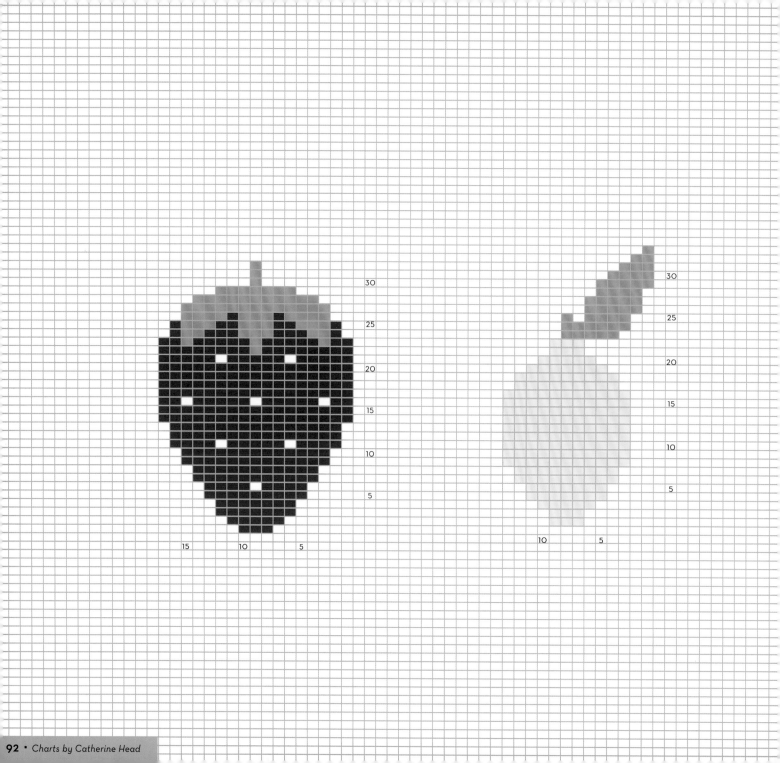

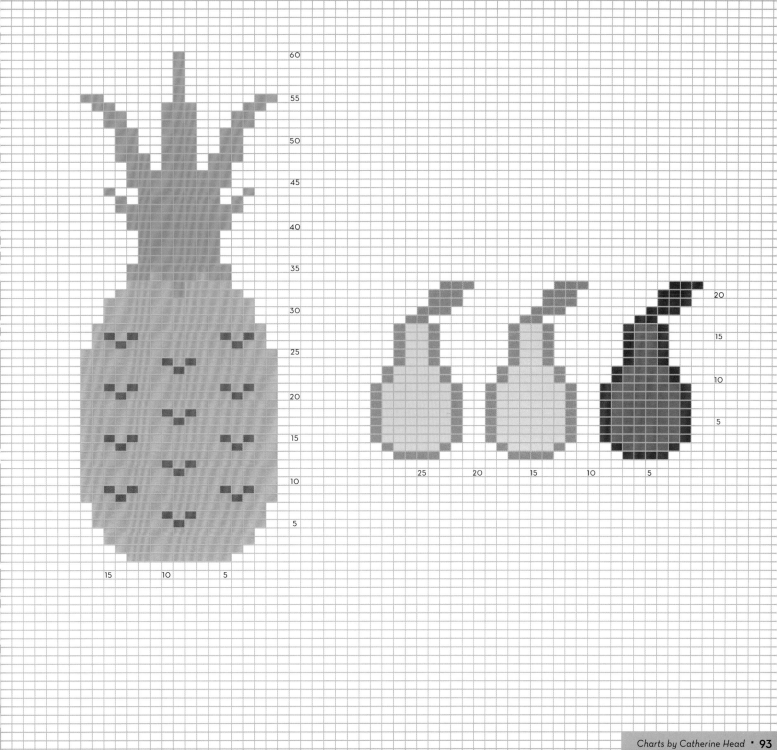

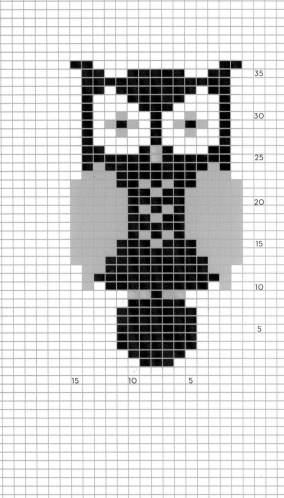

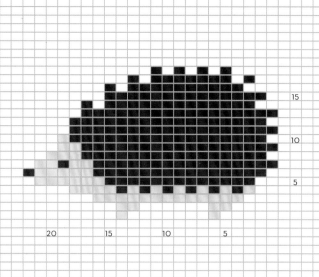

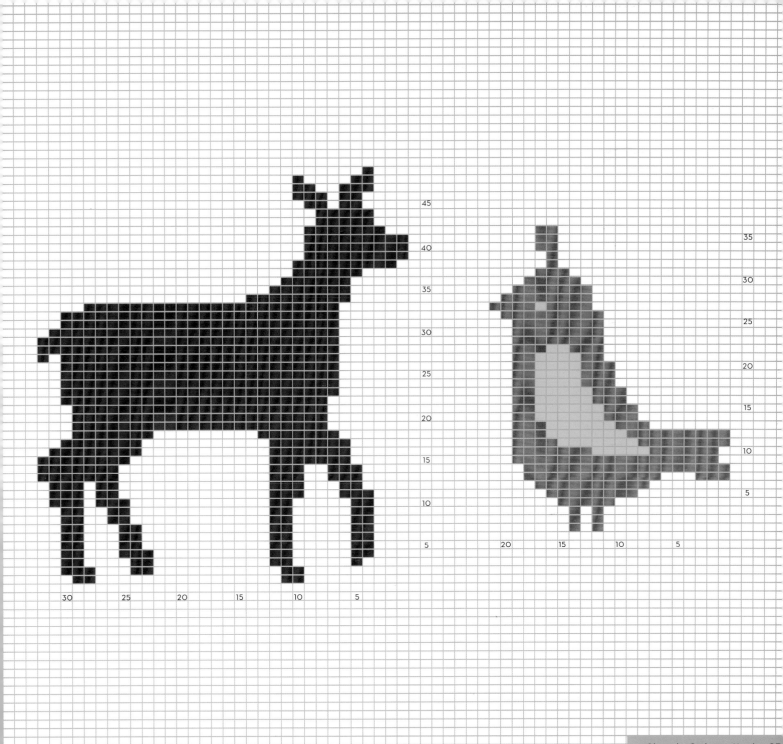

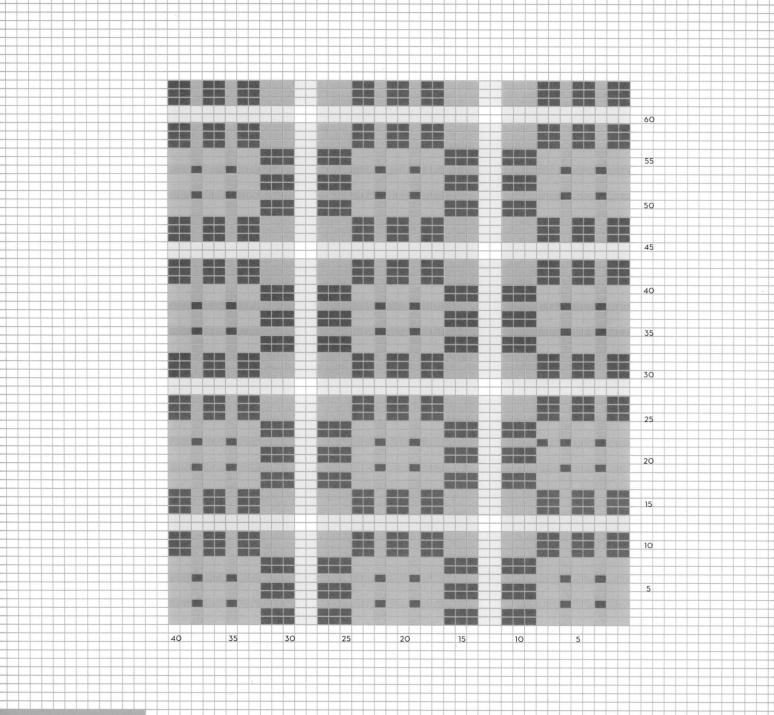

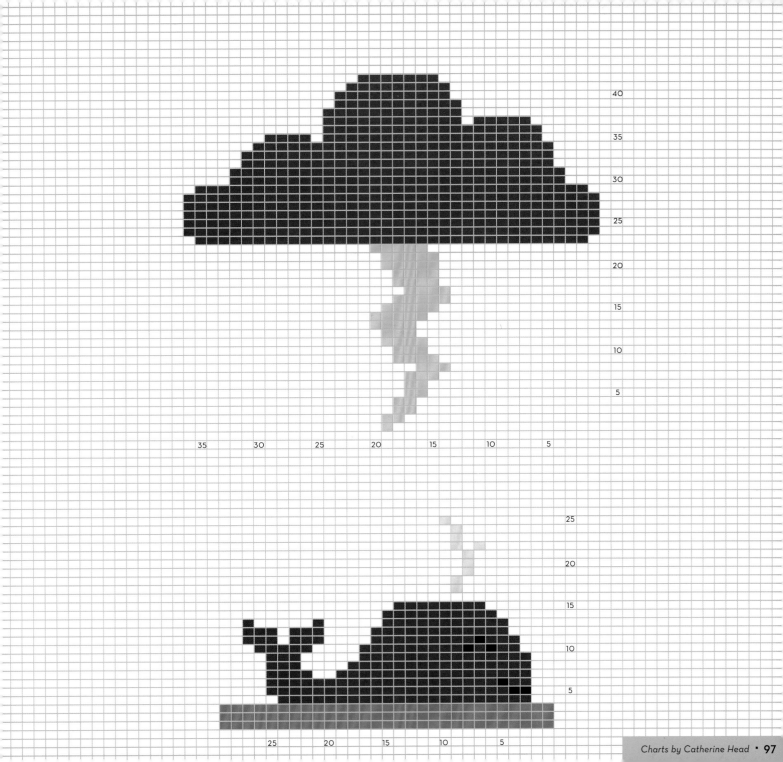

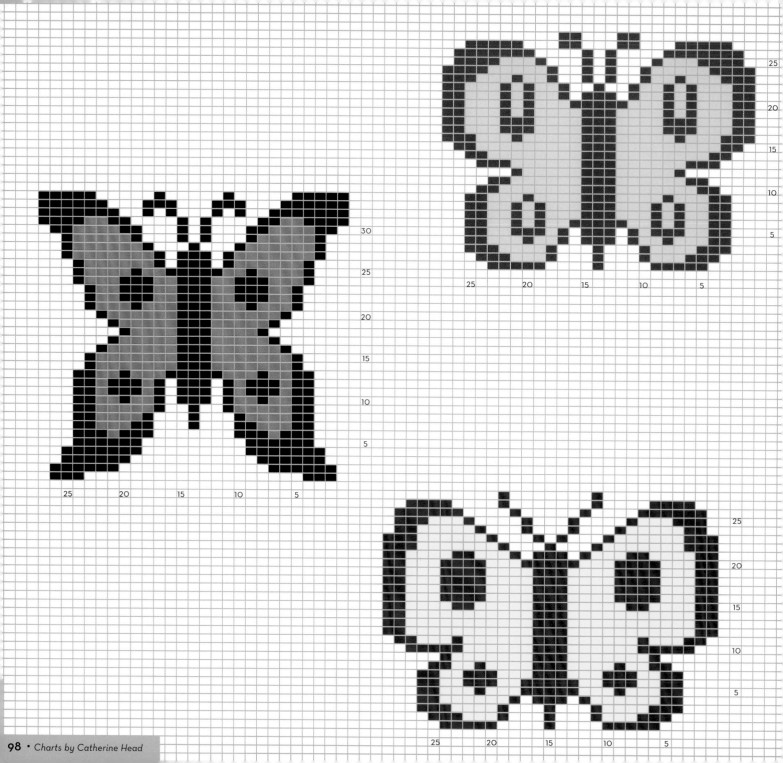

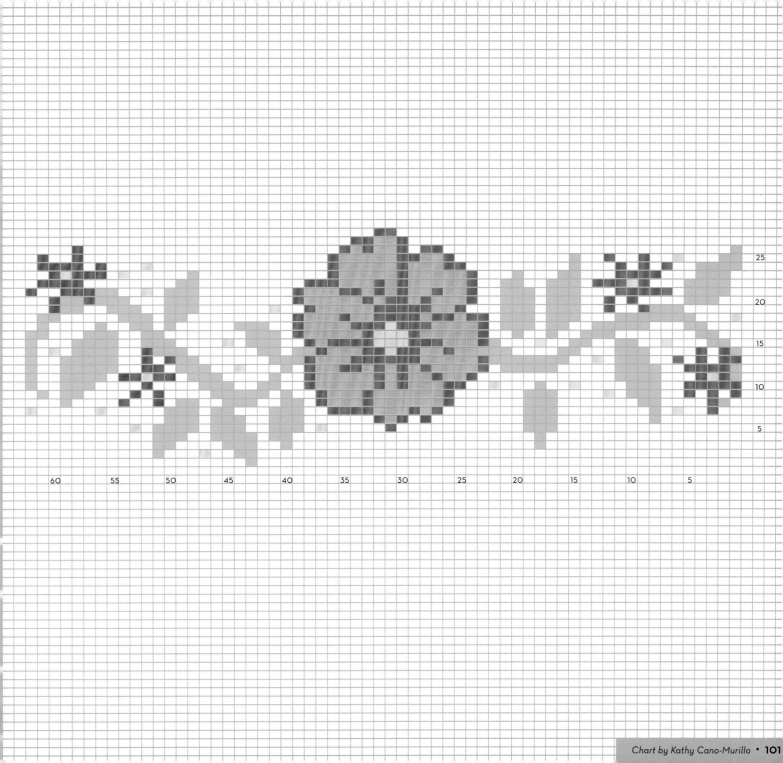

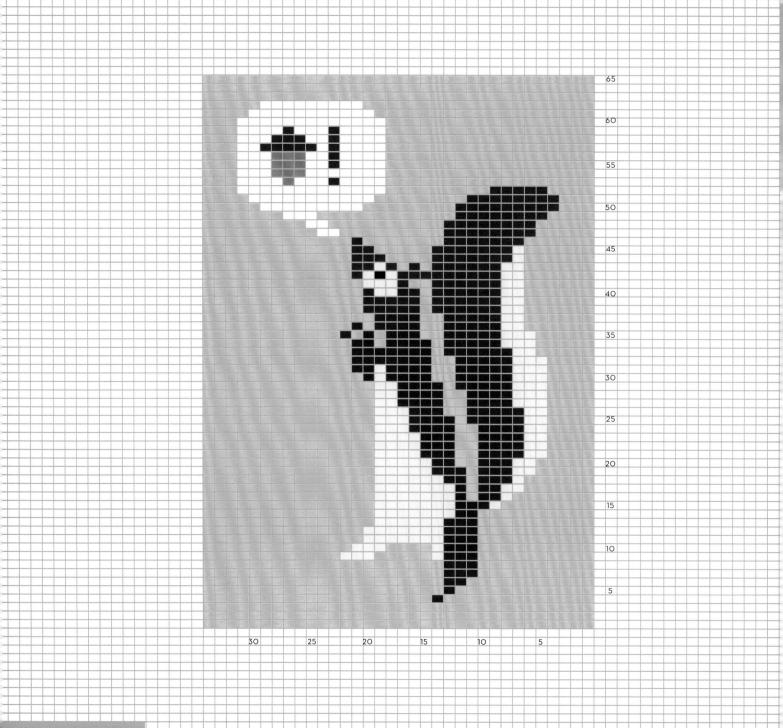

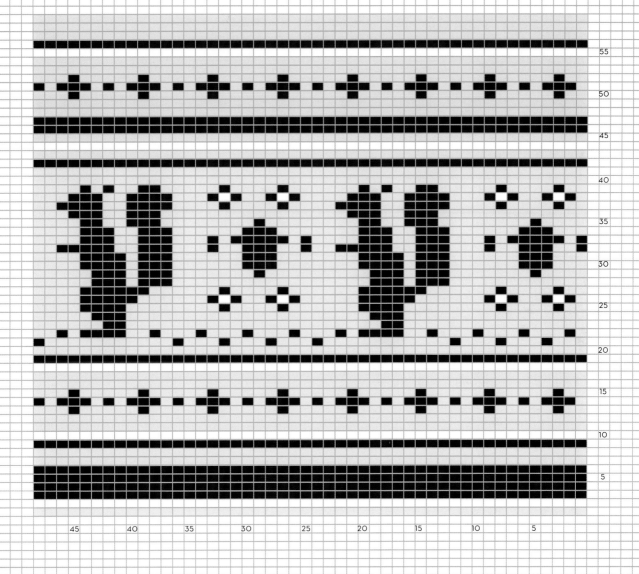

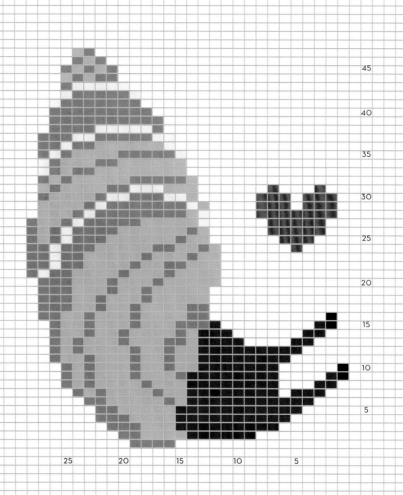

45

40

35

30

25

20

15

10

5

25 20 15 10 5

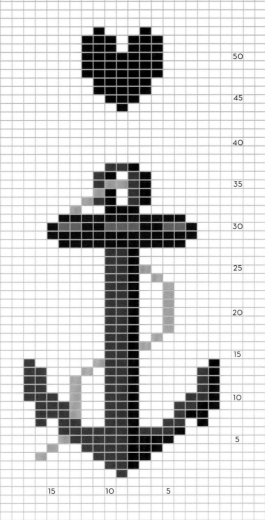

50

45

40

35

30

25

20

15

10

5

15   10   5

55

50

45

40

35

30

25

20

15

10

5

50   45   40   35   30   25   20   15   10   5

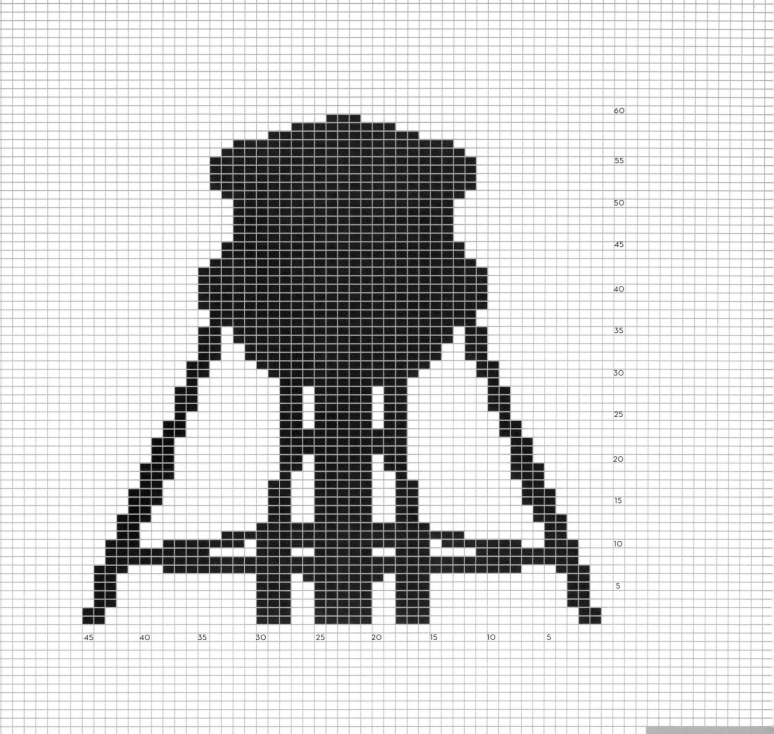

60
55
50
45
40
35
30
25
20
15
10
5

45   40   35   30   25   20   15   10   5

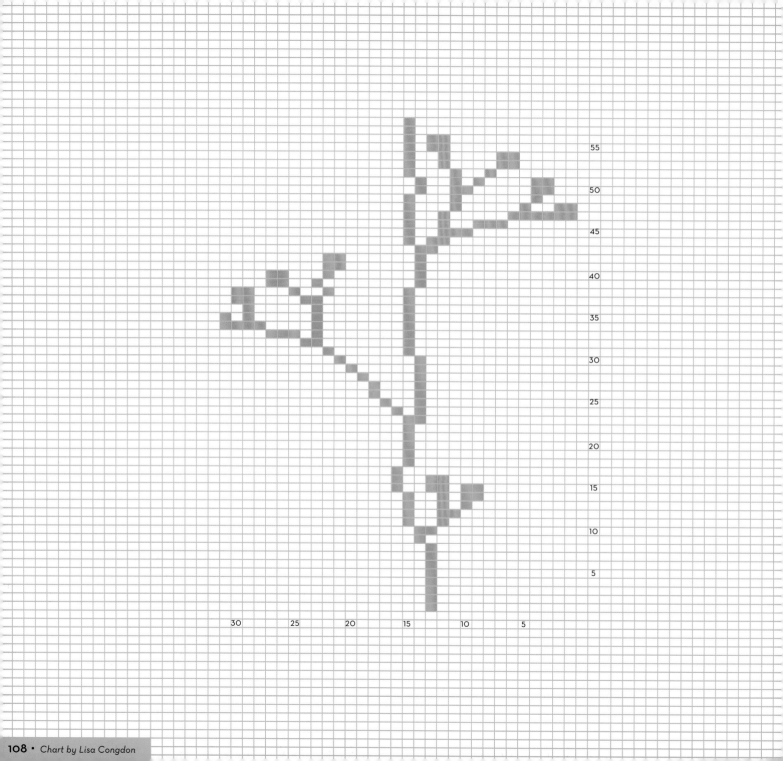

60

55

50

45

40

35

30

25

20

15

10

5

25   20   15   10   5

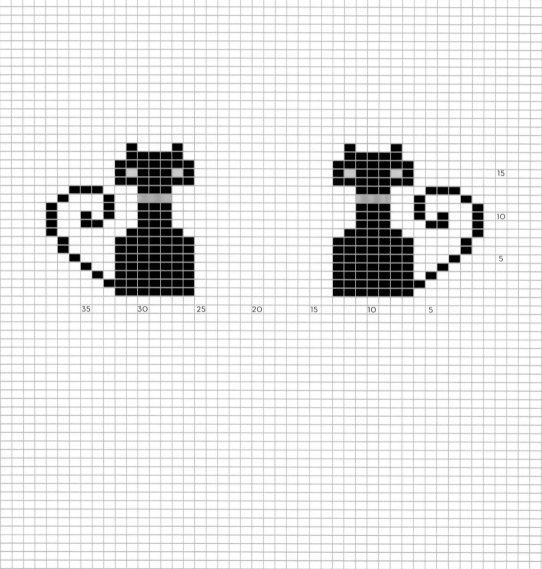

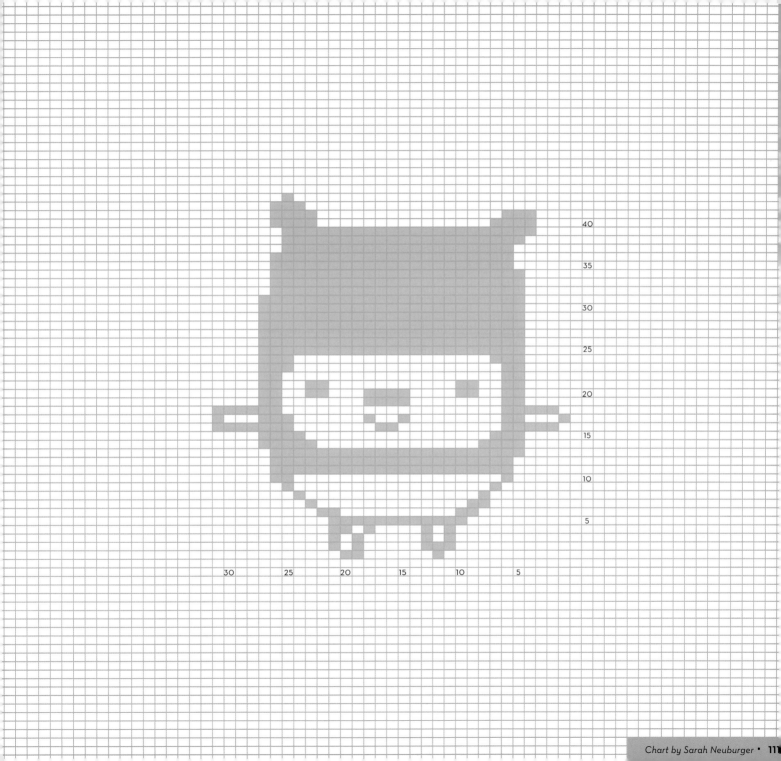

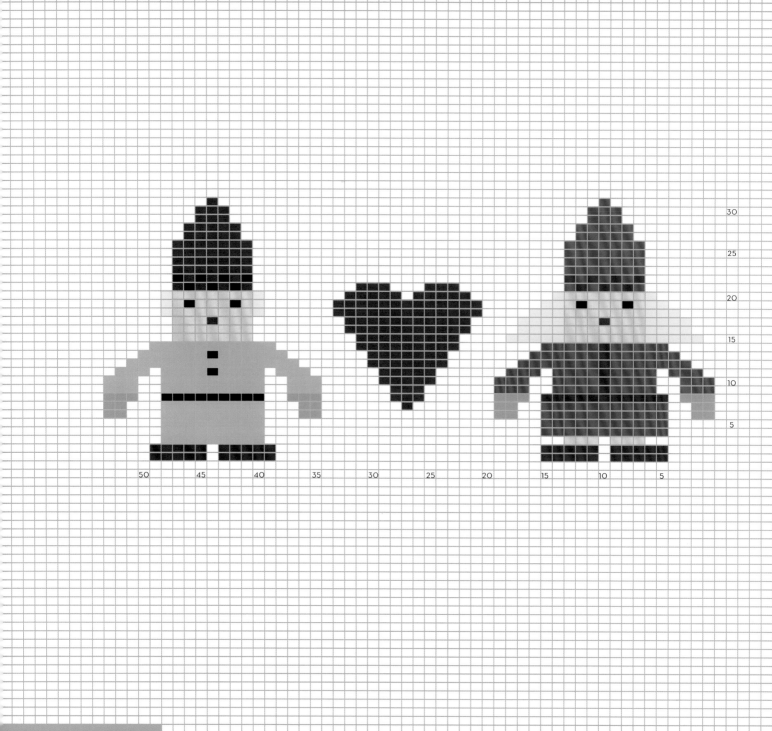

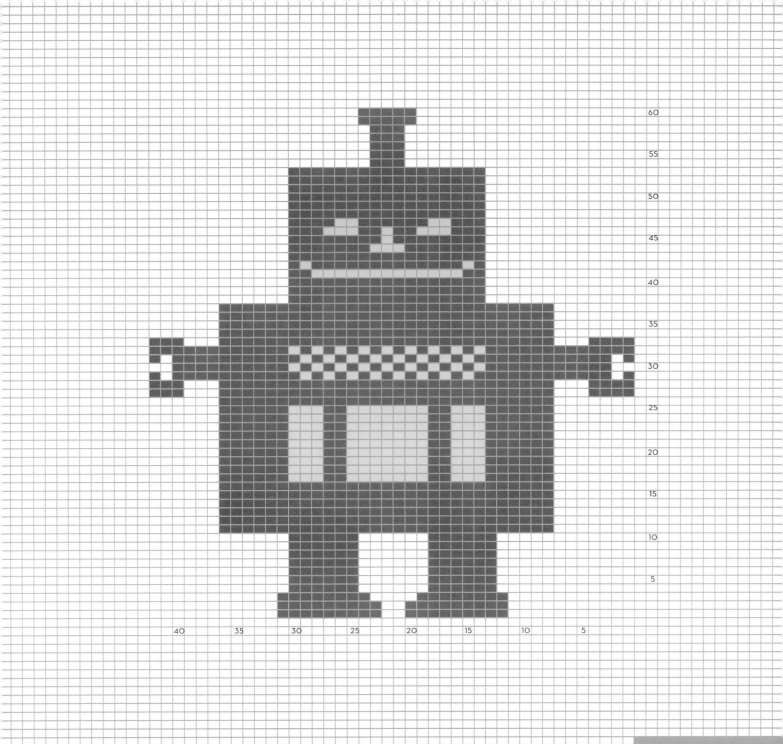

60
55
50
45
40
35
30
25
20
15
10
5

40   35   30   25   20   15   10   5

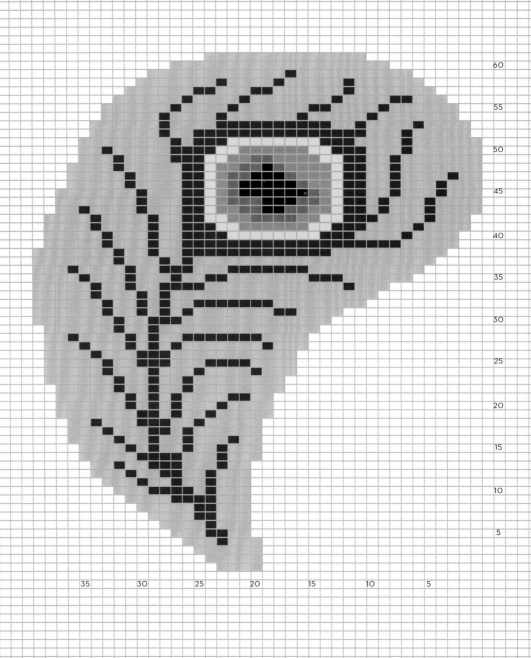

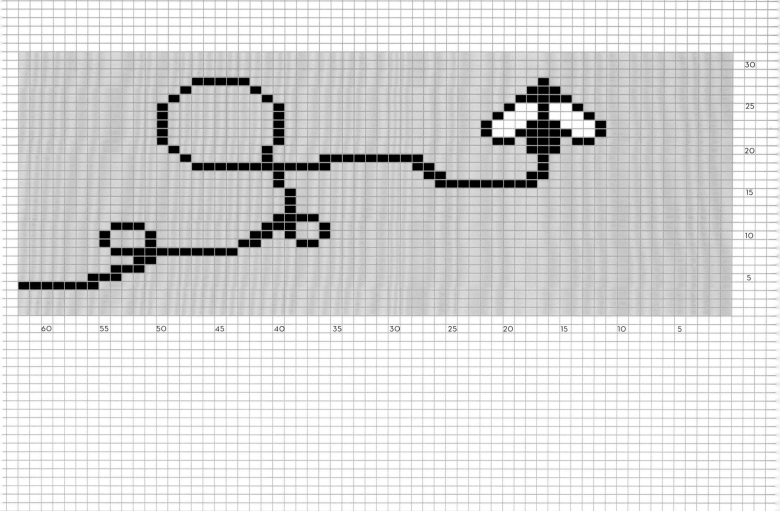

4

ADDITIONAL RESOURCES

GLOSSARY
of Abbreviations and Special Terms

Alt	Alternate.
Beg	Beginning.
Blanket Stitch	Use this stitch to adorn or reinforce the border of any project. To make the stitch, work from left to right. Insert your needle from the front to the back about 1/2 inch above the fabric's edge. With the yarn tail held down, slip the point of the needle over it. Pull through until the stitch is snug against your project. Continue around the edge, keeping the spacing even.
BO	Bind off.
Butterfly	A method of securing lengths of yarn without a bobbin. To make a butterfly, wrap the length of yarn around your index and middle fingers, spread apart. When you have about 8 inches left, flip the remaining yarn upside down to create a loop and wrap it around the yarn. Carefully slip your fingers out of the yarn and pull on the end to secure.
CC	Contrasting color.
CO	Cast on.
Cover stitch	See *duplicate stitch*.
Dec	Decrease.
DPNs	Double-pointed needles.
Duplicate stitch	Embroidery stitch designed to mimic individual knit stitches. Often used to embellish or fix up intarsia motifs. See page 13 for detailed instructions on this technique.
Felting	A method of transforming knit fibers into a sturdier, thicker material. Felting is accomplished by washing knits in hot, soapy water, which causes the fibers to contract and mat together. Felting is traditionally done with wool, but it can also be done with other animal fibers.
Garter Stitch	Knit all rows.
Gm	Gram.
Inc	Increase.
K	Knit.
Kfb	A method of increasing by one stitch. Knit into the front of a knit stitch, pull yarn through without dropping loop off left needle, knit into back of same stitch, then drop loop off left needle.
K2tog	Decrease one stitch by knitting two stitches together.
M1 (make 1)	Increase one stitch by inserting the left needle under the horizontal bar between stitches from back to front, and then knitting it through the front loop.
Mattress Stitch	Use this stitch to seamlessly join two knit pieces. First, match the pieces side by side, right sides facing you with the stitches aligned. Using the same yarn from the project and starting at the left corner, pull the yarn through the middle

	of the first stitch. Be sure to leave a tail about 6-inch long to weave in later. Weave the pieces together from left to right in a vertical zigzag by coming up through the center of the first stitch in each row above the last.
MC	Main color.
1 x 1 Rib	A rib created by alternating knit and purl stitches. To create a 1 x 1 rib over an even number of stitches, (k1, p1) to end of each row. For an uneven number of stitches, (k1, p1), k1 on right-side rows, and (p1, k1), p1 on wrong-side rows.
Oz	Ounce.
P	Purl.
Patt	Pattern.
Pick up	With the right side of your fabric facing you, insert your knitting needle into the gap formed between two stitches. Wrap your yarn around the needle and pull through the gap. Leave yarn on needle and continue in the same manner until you have the desired number of stitches on your needle.
Psso	Pass slipped stitch over.
Rem	Remaining.
RS	Right (public) side.
Sew in ends	With a tapestry needle, thread yarn through the back loops of your knit stitches on the wrong side of the fabric. Sew in one direction for at least an inch, then sew back the other direction for a half inch. Cut off excess yarn.
Skp	Decrease one stitch by slipping one stitch knitwise, knitting the next stitch, then passing the slipped stitch over the stitch just knit.
Sl	Slip.

Sl st	Slip stitch.
SSK	Slip, slip, knit.
Stockinette Stitch (st st)	Knit right-side rows; purl wrong-side rows.
Sts	Stitches.
Tog	Together.
Turn	Turn the work 180 degrees and continue with the next row.
Twist	A method of securing yarn together while working intarsia. To twist, simply lay the first yarn strand over the new yarn strand and continue knitting. See page 12 for detailed instructions on this technique.
Whipstitch	Also known as an overcast stitch. With wrong sides together (right sides out), bring the needle and thread through both pieces of fabric from the back to the front. Move the needle a short way along your edge, and bring the needle back through both pieces from the back to the front again. Continue in this manner. See page 40 for illustrations of this stitch.
Work even	Continue in the same stitch pattern, with no increases or decreases, until further directed.
Wrap	*For right-side rows:* With yarn in front, slip one stitch purlwise, bring yarn to back, place marker on left needle, and return slipped stitch to left needle. *For wrong-side rows:* With yarn in back, slip one stitch purlwise, bring yarn to front, place marker on left needle, and return slipped stitch to left needle.
WS	Wrong side.
* *	Repeat the directions between the stars as indicated in the pattern.
(_)	Repeat the directions between the parentheses as indicated in the pattern.

INTARSIA CHART DESIGNERS

PAGES 79–98

Catherine Head is a graphic designer, stationery geek, and all-around crafter living in Portland, Oregon. Her work can be seen in *Hats, Mittens & Scarves* and *Pretty Pantry Gifts* from Chronicle Books.

PAGES 99–101

Kathy Cano-Murillo, a self-proclaimed art junkie, runs the Web sites CraftyChica.com and ChicanoPopArt.com. She is a TV personality, syndicated newspaper craft columnist, and the author of numerous books including *La Casa Loca* and *Crafty Chica's Art de la Soul.* She lives in Phoenix, Arizona, with her husband, two kids, and four Chihuahuas.

PAGES 102–105

Eunice Moyle is cofounder and creative director of Hello!Lucky, a San Francisco design and letterpress company. An avid knitter, she is particularly fond of using intarsia to apply her vintage-inspired aesthetic and quirky illustrations to her knitting (much to the chagrin of her dog, Simon, who is often the reluctant recipient of nerdy-dad style squirrel-patterned sweaters). She's the co-author of *Handmade Hellos* from Chronicle Books.

SWALLOW, PAGE 106

Alyce Benevides and Jaqueline Milles launched Knit-Head, a line of punk-rock knitwear, in 2005. They operate out of New York City and online at www.knit-head.com. In May 2007, Chronicle Books published their book, *Pretty in Punk: 25 Punk, Rock, and Goth Knitting Projects.*

WATER TOWER, PAGE 107

Graphic designer Ed Roth founded Stencil1 in Brooklyn in 2005. In addition to Stencil1, Ed currently consults with various advertising agencies and post-houses such as R/GA, Homestead Editorial, and Edgeworx. He's the author of *Stencil 101* from Chronicle Books. You can visit Ed at www.stencil1.com.

VINE, PAGE 108

San Francisco mixed-media artist, illustrator, and designer Lisa Congdon works in several mediums, including paper collage, screen-printing, India ink, and paint. She is mostly self-taught and uses her lack of training to her advantage. Instead of following refined technique, she works with her own sense of color, composition, and design as her guide. You can visit Lisa at www.lisacongdon.com.

JELLYFISH, PAGE 109

Jenny Hart is an artist and designer who revitalized the interest in embroidery by founding Sublime Stitching in 2001. She is the author of *Stitch-It Kit, Sublime Stitching,* and *Sublime Stitching Craft Pad,* all from Chronicle Books. Jenny lives and works in Austin, Texas, where she is a member of the infamous Austin Craft Mafia.

BLACK CATS, PAGE 110

Diane Gilleland, aka Sister Diane, blogs and podcasts at CraftyPod.com. She also runs DIYAlert.com, a Web site for crafty things in Portland, Oregon.

Creature, page 111

Sarah Neuburger thinks there simply cannot be anything cooler than knitting drawings. She also thinks making her drawings into stamps, stationery, and housewares is the best job going, hands down. You can see all her business tom-foolery over at her online shop The Small Object, www.thesmallobject.com.

Tulip Tree, page 112

Denyse Schmidt has been designing and making quilts since 1996. Denyse's quilts have been featured in *Denyse Schmidt Quilts* from Chronicle Books and in numerous publications including the *New York Times; Martha Stewart Living; People; O, The Oprah Magazine;* and *Time.*

Starflower, page 113

Shannon Okey is the voice behind the craft blog knitgrrl.com, *The Pillow Book* from Chronicle Books, and several other fabric-related books. She has appeared on a number of television shows, including *Knitty Gritty, Uncommon Threads,* and *Crafters Coast to Coast.* For this intarsia graph, she re-created a motif from Starflower Tiles fabric designed by Amy Butler, an author and celebrated designer of textiles, fashion products, stationery goods, and home accessories.

My Gnomies, page 114

Andrea Tomlinson is a knitting librarian who lives and works in Pennsylvania.

RobotKnit, page 115

Aoife Clifford lives in Melbourne, Australia, where she enjoys knitting, drawing, and writing.

Peacock Paisley, page 116

Alice Merlino is the woman behind the craft blog futuregirl.com. She lives in Philadelphia.

The Fly, page 117

Manuela Tinoco is a teacher who learned knitting as a child by observing her neighbor in Portugal, where she lives.

Yoga Aum, page 118

Tracy Jen is a knitter, crocheter, and stitcher living in the San Francisco Bay Area.

INDEX

RESOURCES

Chart-Making Resources

Actual-size graph papers:
www.tata-tatao.to/knit/matrix/e-index.html

Cochenille Stitch Painter:
www.cochenille.com/stitch.html

knitPro software:
www.microrevolt.org/knitPro

Sweaterscapes knitting charts:
sweaterscapes.com/lcharts3.htm

Yarn resources

Brown Sheep Company: www.brownsheep.com
Elann: www.elann.com
Knit Picks: www.knitpicks.com
Lion Brand Yarn: www.lionbrand.com
Unwind Yarn: unwindyarn.com

Magazines

Interweave Knits
Knit.1
Rowan
Vogue Knitting

Knitting Web sites

Café Press: www.cafepress.com
Craftster: www.craftster.org
Craft Yarn Council of America: www.craftyarncouncil.com
Knitty: knitty.com
Mag Knits: www.magknits.com
Ravelry: www.ravelry.com
The Knitting Guild Association: tkga.com

Other resources

See Eunny Knit: Eunny Jang's wet-blocking tutorial,
"Block Me, Amadeus"
www.eunnyjang.com/knit/2006/05/block_me_amadeus_1.html